D0331550

Lessons and Stories from the Culinary World's Elite

MAKING
THE *Cut*

WHAT SEPARATES THE BEST FROM THE REST

CHRIS HILL

An Imprint of PacesFerry Press

ATLANTA

SECOND EDITION

Cover Art designed by Mathaniel Chesson.

Front Cover Photography by Leslie Woodward.

Back Cover Photography by Beethoven Awit Jr.

Edited by Laura DeVries

Library of Congress Cataloging-in-Publication Data

Hill, Chris.

Making the Cut / Chris Hill. 1st ed. May, 2016

Paperback ISBN: 978-0-692-68117-6

10 9 8 7 6 5 4 3 2

To my family, especially my parents – Dad and Cheryl.

To you Christina, I really don't know where or, more importantly, who I would be without you in my life.

And to you, Mom, and the book you never got to finish. Ever since you left this earth, I've been dreaming of acknowledging you in a book – I hope you're somewhere smiling.

CONTENTS

FOREWORD

Early in my career, I lied in order to get a job. Several times.

It could have been any career, really; plumber, carpenter, doctor, lawyer, banker. If my experience in the culinary industry – a highly technical and incredibly stressful field – was any indication of the stressors specific to being a beginner of any craft or art, I suspect that other people may have felt similarly suspect; fronting up fraudulently just to get one's foot in the door, trying to earn their bones.

'Lied' may be a bit harsh; "Several times in my youth, I misrepresented myself in order to secure a position of employment." Sounds a bit more accurate, but nonetheless dubious.

I was stuck between a rock and a hard place. After high school, college seemed out of reach as did culinary school. With the specter of a stint in the military shadowing my every career choice, I enrolled in the School of Hard Knocks and started hustling on the street, building a skill set from scratch in a few knock-down kitchens. I was a demon on the grill but a beginner on sauté. I wanted to earn more, learn more and at that time the only way to do that was to want it more than anyone else on the line. I pulled muscles in my neck looking over the raised shoulders of sous chefs and chefs, trying to get a glimpse of the deeper purposes of the magic they were creating. Their backs always seemed to be screening my view of their skills or knowledge that they had and were protecting; ones that I lacked and coveted.

No one, up to that point, had been willing to explain or demonstrate to me techniques and processes that seemed like sorcery to my inexperienced eyes. How does an egg hold an emulsion, and what the hell is an emulsion anyway?

I was often left confused, mystified and more determined than ever to learn as much as I could about cooking, and how to be successful at it. But since no one was talking I was left on my own to figure it out, armed with only an intense desire and a tattered copy of Paul Bocuse's "French Cooking" to fill in the blanks.

"Can you clean a beef tenderloin?" I was asked

"Oui chef", I would say, then try to hide the garish silver skin trimmings in the garbage can, under a box.

"Can you bake a Genoise Cake?"

"Oui chef", I would reply, then throw out the first six while scouring the recipe to see where I'd gone wrong in the process.

"Can you clean St Peter's Fish?

"Oh, Oui chef!!" I exclaimed as I wondered what a St. Peter's Fish was. It's John Dory by the way and man oh man, what a pain in the ass it is to clean!!

I became very good at learning quickly; my continued employment frequently depended on my capacity to bridge the gap between what I knew and what was possible in the shortest distance necessary. There weren't many other options open to me. Back then I only had a dream – the dream of the dance.

When I was 15, I worked as a dishwasher in a family restaurant in Hammond Indiana; The Big Wheel, which at that time had a stainless steel ticket wheel in the pass between the kitchen and the counter stools. The kitchen was run by a beautifully gregarious woman by the name of Artelia White or "T" as she preferred. Her considerable girth was surpassed only by the enormity of her heart and good nature. Her compatriot was a thin, severe woman who was as silent and unassuming as T was jovial and commanding.

On a particular Saturday night, I was hurrying to replenish plates and silverware in the server area, when I passed by the doorway to the kitchen and was struck dumb by what I saw or thought I saw; my spirit quickened, my heart caught in my throat. I watched as T and her coworker handled the rush, smoothly and without drama. They worked in concert with one another, in perfect silent synchronicity; never bumping, pushing or jostling. It was an orchestrated symphony of movement, sound, steam and steel; their fluid dance together was once of the most beautiful things I had ever seen.

"Whatever that is," I said to myself, "I'm gonna get me some."

I was roused out of my reverie by someone shouting for more clean glasses, but upon picking my jaw up off the ground I was left haunted by that dance; my dream of that dance would push me forward for the rest of my culinary career. To create or be part of a perfect sell, a perfect shift with a kick ass crew; an organic machine spitting out art and beauty to a chorus of angels and heavy metal music.

That dream, however persuasive, was not my reality early in my career; I studied, I lied, I learned, I worked my ass off and finally, I made it by all standards used by my contemporaries.

Or had I? I had broken my back (twice, actually), sacrificed two marriages, was never really present for my kids, and suffered through bouts of substance abuse, addiction and depression. Was this how my dream would end, with squandered promise and wasted relationships?

Had I gained the world only to lose myself?

I took myself out of the game for a bit, even left the country, in order to get some perspective and to be able to come to some conclusion about what I wanted my life to be. It was easier at first to make a list of the things I didn't want my life to be about, but eventually I settled on one thing that had the potential to motivate me past my previous 'set points' and it had me digging deeper and looking harder at my choices up until then: I wanted to be in contribution.

I wanted to be in contribution to the culinary field and, more importantly, in service to the reason why I feel in love with this business in the first place: those wonderful, sometimes wacky personalities that make up our fraternity, brother and sisterhood.

I wanted to assist, if I could, those coming up after me; lighten their burden a bit, hip them to the mistakes I had made so that they could make different choices, lead different lives than I had. My instincts, gut – whatever you're comfortable calling it – had been trying to tell me for a long time that there was another way; another way to lead and motivate. I knew that there must be a way to impact the lives of others better than how I had been doing it, after all my results up until then had been lackluster, to say the least.

I started doing some research; started a radio show and started writing some compelling articles about the industry. Words being words, I decided to put my ass on the line and start living it; I re-inserted myself into the field that I loved so much and started to advocate where I was and for what I thought might be possible.

I started putting into practice that which I had only read or heard theories about. I was having 1000 conversations a day. I started speaking less and listening more, and the more I heard, the more I was encouraged. There were other professionals out there who, for reasons all their own, had come to similar conclusions and weren't waiting around for someone else to shift things.

Two years ago on a blustery winter's evening I read a blog post that I had come across from a guy whom I hadn't known before, Chef Chris Hill. "Dear Chefs – An Open Letter" was an entertaining read but it was also thoroughly compelling; to the point, kind, considerate, but also blunt. I immediately felt compelled to share it with my listeners and anyone I knew. I printed a copy and put it on our communal bulletin board in the kitchen, highlighting passages.

I read it on the show and included links to the original post; job done, mission accomplished – or so I thought. Several months later I received an email from Chris, thanking me for including it in the show. I'm still not sure how he ever came across the show or the fact that I was so stricken by it. Nevertheless, it was an unlikely start to what's evolved into a wonderful friendship marked by honesty, vulnerability and good humor.

Yes, we share some of the same sensibilities when it comes to living and leading in life, but when Chris speaks there is a resonance in his words that carries with them the possibility of shifting a culture for the better. I could always learn from others a better way to filet a fish or how to shave a few points off of my food cost, however, there were few industry voices advocating a different way of being, as a chef, leader or human being; until Chris decided to share his story with the world, that is.

Here in this book, Chris has gathered together some incredible insight from some of today's best chefs, thought leaders and hospitality professionals for just one purpose: to discover that which is so elusive in today's marketplace: success with integrity.

This is more than a book about culinary insight; this is a book for anyone who wants to discover what sets excellence apart from the pack, what it takes to 'Make the Cut' from mediocrity – personally and professionally.

Adam M. Lamb, Chef Life Radio

∞ MAKING THE CUT ∞

INTRODUCTION

My breath isn't quite visible, however, its heat seems to be the
only thing keeping me warm in my windowless office, aside from
the occasional ring of scalding coffee steam sifting my way. It's
black and stronger than I'd prefer, but just what I'd need for
another long graveyard shift at the restaurant that had long since
closed for the night. The restaurant is quiet. No banging pans.
No customers and not even employees or even music playing in
the dining room – just the hum of the hood in the open kitchen
and the cranky, about to keel-over-and-die convection oven. It's
on its last leg. On occasion, I'll wander up to the kitchen line and
check on the two pigs roasting in the convection oven at a very
low heat. Lining the bottom of the oven is a trough of wood
chips, into which the pig fat slowly drips over the course of the
night. This is far from any sort of ideal smoking technique, but it
seems to work when constrained by a small kitchen and limited
resources.

During the days and even early nights the temperature in the
office is nice this time of year; it's the same time of year that
equates to just barely barren trees and chimneys begin coughing
smoke into the night sky at dusk. Back in the restaurant, fresh off
of the kitchen line – beat up, dirty and sweaty, the office in most
restaurants is a welcomed respite for a tired chef to rest their legs.
Restaurant kitchens don't have chairs. Or stools. The closest
thing you're likely to find to appropriate seating as a kitchen
worker during a long, hot shift is an upside-down milk carton

stacked in the alleyway behind the restaurant, right next to a bin of half-smoked, choked-down cigarette butts.

The office has plenty of seats, and though they are mostly beaten up rolling chairs that never seem to steady their height quite right, the fact that they exist is enough for anyone on the closing bits of a twelve hour double to seek refuge there.

It's hard to describe the relief that settles into your legs as you rest your feet for the first time in hours. Aside from a cold beer, a comfortable seat is the next best thing to a nice long soak in a steaming hot bath. Unfortunately, the years under your belt in the kitchen are directly proportional to the number of pain reliever tablets to be ingested post-shift. Your age really hits you the following morning when your achy bones don't want to budge from bed, especially if you decided to knock off a few rounds of drinks with the crew after work.

Next weekend we've got two caterings and a full house both nights, plus my business partner invited a group of friends, of which he'll probably comp, into the private dining room right at seven-thirty. What the hell is he thinking? He's not damnit. He's not, because he's not the one pumping food out for the entire restaurant, plus readying an off-site catering for seventy. With his twenty-five dumb-ass friends most likely insisting on ordering off the full menu, that should set a nice tone of chaos for the remainder of the evening. Once you get behind, it's almost impossible to catch back up. Fuck. Fridays are hard, but Saturdays take it out of me. Three heavy-hitting days on my feet, hell, I feel like I'm getting too old for this at thirty-three. Only thirty-three. If there is anything I've learned over my decade grinding it out, it's that the industry can take a toll on you. It'll knock you down, run you over and kick you in the gut as you rise to your feet, and if you aren't careful, it can get the best of you. It's ubiquitous in this industry, and it's why we see so many of our colleagues falling into the same old story of getting hammered after work and then wrecking their cars. If they do, let's just hope there isn't any weed or coke in the glove-box this time, because chances are you'll need him or her on the line this weekend – stuck behind a set of bars in a jail cell is the last thing the restaurant needs. I've been there before, I'm just grateful I never hurt anyone, myself or my vehicle.

When I became a restaurant owner and eventually grew into what would be the executive chef of the restaurant, I soon realized I'd be taking the biggest pay cut of my life. I was making more money a week working as a twelve year old at Camp Grasshopper, shoveling six year old kids around for the summer, making thirty-five bucks a week. Those first few years were long, really damn long. I'll never forget walking that first check over to the bank after a busy Friday lunch service, looking at the check and thinking about how many unpaid hours were stuffed into this one, $750 check that represented three years of unwavering hard work.

So, for those first years of not only not getting paid, but actually having to put money into the restaurant, you can probably imagine I'd need to supplement this expensive habit of mine that we commonly refer to as a restaurant. Unfortunately, this habit also included responsibilities such as payroll, ordering, rent checks, menu creation, staff management and the list goes on. I think I could have opened my own bank with the ubiquitous overdraft fees that rolled through in those first sub break-even winters. We made it through, unlike many others and turned the corner, ever so slightly, but still had a job working another forty hours a week, in order to make ends meet.

I felt owed something. My hard work, dedication to the mission and just by being a good guy left me feeling entitled to a certain level of success that didn't exist in my career, yet. This left me bitter and, in many ways, resentful. I had a relationship that was falling apart – my girlfriend couldn't understand my life and why I'd chosen this path and neither could my family back home in Atlanta. It didn't make sense to them, naturally so, but if I could somehow map what success looks like in the kitchen – what it means and how we can get there, then maybe I could create it;

not only myself, but for other people in the industry, and in doing so, help everyone better understand this crazy industry a lot of us have chosen to and are proud to be a part of.

So, I started writing this book, with my own preconceived ideas of what success looked like – they have changed slightly, and that has happened through interviewing dozens of my contemporaries, all of whom are far more accomplished than myself. As I started formulating this hypothesis of sorts, I started actively pursuing speaking engagements, in order to bring some awareness about the book, myself, and my mission.

I was recently giving a talk at American Culinary Federation that was based on a number of interviews with these prized chefs – it's their stories that are detailed throughout the book. As it came to a close, I was given a warm round of applause and offered audience members the opportunity to keep the conversation going down-front after. A line formed in front of me, I drank a quick swig from my water bottle to fight the cotton mouth that had developed over the course of my talk, and as I approached the crowd, a young lady stood with auburn hair waited sternly in front. She was maybe twenty or so and I assume was working her way through culinary school. I reached my hand out to shake hers, which were wrapped tightly around her body. They didn't budge and she looked up at me unimpressed, like I had just attempted to start a fight during recess on the playground in elementary school. Subtly, she just barely met my eyes with hers.

"I came to your talk because, based on the description, I was under the impression that this was going to be an inspiring and uplifting talk, but I think it was trash, all you did was talk about how shitty chef life is and I just felt more discouraged every step of the way, until you stopped talking..."

"I'm so sorr-," I started, and she was gone.

I've given TEDx talks, plenty of TV appearances and spoken to various groups in various settings, but this was the very first person to offer me feedback on a presentation for an event that was focused on my target audience. I was blindsided. My goal and mission was just the opposite of what she took away from it.

Perhaps she was right though, in a sense, I hadn't started formulating this book at that point, and I'm sure bits and pieces of my thoughts and stories were somewhat disjointed, lacking cohesion. Even though it was just one person, it was one impressionable person that I'd lost – I guess you can't win 'em all, but it sure feels nice to think you can. I've lost various others, both quite literally and figuratively, as well. I lost Blake and Chad, but in a different ways that you'll read about in the proceeding pages – they seem to be martyrs of sorts for this grueling, stressful industry that's suffered for far too long. The nameless young lady, who I assumed was in culinary school, I had lost her, but maybe not for good. Perhaps I could frame things in a way that made sense to her. I needed to exemplify a mindset that she could buy into that would, in a sense, mitigate the risk of pouring her heart and soul into this industry that's so notorious for swallowing up people, families and communities, whole.

That day, when I first gave that talk to a room full of chefs, was a good one for the most part, and further opened my eyes to the concept of success and how we all desperately want it. Often, we just don't know how to get there. You've just got to learn to fight through some of the bad, figure out some of the things that don't work, to figure out the ones that do, and as the great Tony Robbins says, look around for the clues, because success leaves them behind – everywhere they go.

This book is the clues. A recipe, of sorts. At least I hope.

The journey within these pages is a look into the great chefs of the world, who've been generous enough to share their stories (the good parts and the bad), so that we can all better understand what success looks like for the greatest culinary professionals of our time. What are they doing differently than everyone else? OR, what are they NOT doing that everyone else is? It turns out, the same themes threaded themselves through the various stories of these impressive individuals who have created success for themselves and their communities, but more than that, it seemed to carry over into their personal lives. These are successful people, not just successful chefs. It definitely takes surrounding yourself with people that you respect and appreciate, and then nurturing those relationships, but at the end of the day – it's an inside job. Success starts with who you are, who you want to be, and how you show up every single day. The way each of us answers the important questions of our lives dictates whether or not we are moving close to or farther away from success.

It's not easy, and every day is a challenge, especially if you're committed to doing your best work and being better than you were the day before. While my story is riddled with failures, disappointments and not quite having my chef story pan out as I'd hoped thus far, the book isn't about me – it's about them and the lessons we can apply to our lives – every single day.

Damn. I almost forgot about the pigs roasting away up front.

They are long overdue for a good basting. I can smell their crispy skin from here, and that wondrous odor of that smoky wood will occupy the restaurant for hours.

I'm grateful for restaurants and, more specifically, the kitchen.

I'm grateful for this industry, as it's a big part of what has shaped the man that I've become.

I'm grateful for the chefs you'll soon read about – their stories and their generosity.

There has to be a better way, though. I'm hoping you'll find that here – I sure as hell did.

CHRIS HILL

*"The ultimate failure is success
without fulfillment."*
TONY ROBBINS

DANCING IN THE FIRE

Just getting off the line after another long day on the line, it feels pretty damn good to look around and see that all tickets, which were once hanging in the expo window, are now gone. They've been stabbed and the manager working expo smiles into the kitchen, "good push, kitchen." The crew steps out of the back door and enjoys the blistery fall breeze of the Florida panhandle. It feels even better when you've been standing in the heat of the 120 degree kitchen for the last six hours. There are fourteen of them running the show, dancing in perfect sync to the beat of the kitchen gods, but this kind of dynamic isn't built overnight, or even over a few weeks, but, in this circumstance, over the course of the busy summer that was now winding down. Fourteen men and women pumping out food all summer as efficiently as they can – it's a thing of beauty, almost hard to fathom unless you've seen it first hand or really been a part of it. For an outsider, it might appear as though a bunch of misfits are bouncing around the kitchen, with no real order. Reaching for this. Ducking behind him, for this, and passing behind her for any number of reasons. But it's all done with thought, at least in a good kitchen. During those gangbuster months when the tourists flood to the white beaches of the Gulf, the kitchen pumps out up to ten grand an hour, sending delicious food to the 700 or so seats that are scattered throughout the restaurant, inside and out – that's a hell of a lot of food. It's good food too. Sales fluctuate during peak season, but on average range from seven to nine grand per hour. When you break it down, that's a hell of a lot of food coming out of each cook's station. Some make eight or nine bucks an hour, while others, the most senior of the crew, will find themselves topping out at fifteen. Let's say the average wage of a high volume establishment like this is twelve an hour, which is on the higher end. Assuming that and an average of forty hours in a week, that breaks down to just under 25 grand a year. That's not enough. It's not enough for most, and it's not enough for him.

He has three children from two different mothers and has never been one to succeed in relationships. Maybe it's the long hours that take a toll on us kitchen workers and our relationships. Maybe it's the substance abuse. He's been off and on for years and is unfortunately on right now, as he writes me this letter at 3 AM.

"I'm 27 and have been in the trenches for 12 years and I've never seen anyone that has a meaningful, fulfilled relationship. Hell, my son's mother and I lasted 3 months after he was born. She had no problem with me kicking ass at two jobs and making bank while she was pregnant, but when he was born, I got a salary gig with insurance and was home more and that made her happy. Still, she never understood why I wanted to shower after a 12 hour shift in the restaurant, instead of walking in the door to grab the baby so she could go outside and smoke. Most of the guys I've been through hell with on the line have baby mommas, ex-wives, or are single and go about their business, banging a waitress or bartender here and there. The only marriages I've seen that have stood the test of time are chefs that have a wife that doesn't work. These chefs make enough and work enough to provide for their families and their wives don't have jobs, whether it be because they would never see each other or their wife is happy being a stay-at-home mom. We are a breed that NOBODY understands except our comrades at work and the waitresses through the window that wanna take us home. Non-industry people don't get us. We want to be with these people instead of waitresses and bartenders because their world is intriguing and "comfortable" but it seems statistically impossible. We stand over the fire, wield knives, communicate by yelling across the kitchen, hurt ourselves by lifting heavy shit wrong, burn ourselves and sell our souls to get through the rush some nights because that shift beer, a cigarette, talking shit, and some ass before bed is what we want rather than catching a TV show at prime time after a "long day at the office." I wouldn't survive a day in a cubicle. There's no motivation. No dance. No pressure except some suit saying he needs the

results of the recent audit sent to him and the fax machine is broken. "Oh no! Not the fax machine!" I'm thinking my homeboy on sauté just got busted for possession and he's the badass, so we gotta get him bailed out before Friday night, we're gonna need him. And now the fryer is shooting fire from the exhaust, the grill-side reach-in isn't holding temp, and the salad bitch just about lost his middle finger because he didn't tuck his fingers chopping green onions.

I've had a few drinks, plus feeling pretty good, except I'm kinda depressed. My baby's mom hasn't dropped my kid off to me in two months even though a judge signed my custody papers saying I have equal custody and that was nearly two years ago. My life is in shambles bro; two failed relationships with three kids and this second failed attempt at family life has me starting again at square one in family court. Maybe my crazy hours or misunderstood work ethic or lack of patience ruined my relationships, but dammit, I've got 5 cooks that I'm close with and about 5 servers that've been there for me through it all. They're my support system. Working in the fire is my release from the stress of the world. Sounds macabre, but it's real shit.

It's real, the dark side: addiction, alcoholism, failed relationships, and how the drive and passion can consume you to the point where you only feel safe around the felons, addicts, and heathens of the world. They don't judge you; they understand, respect you and appreciate you because you kick ass with them, day in and day out. Other people won't ever understand why we surround ourselves with these people, because they will never have the privilege of knocking elbows, sweating, bleeding, and celebrating the end of a $50,000 shift! Why a privilege? Because it doesn't matter if you're Black, White, Latino, or Vietnamese. All that matters is that you can get it done and if you can dance with you *Chris – you can dance with you – is that correct? in the fire. It's the one place you can learn cuss words in three languages and shoot the shit with a guy fresh out of prison and NOBODY is judged for it. Our world is the melting pot of miscreants, heathens and scallywags and anyone is welcome, if you have thick skin and calloused hands. Does everyone have the best morals and values? No! Do you want your kids to witness what goes on at work? No! Are you automatically guilty by association? Hell no, but we love it. Yet, sadly, no one understands but us.

I read it, and a second time. And then again. There was so much to it. Not just the macabre, brashness of it all, but in a lot of ways, it was pretty damn accurate. It's unfortunate, but almost an understanding, that amongst a group of cooks there will be a few with a criminal past and there are most likely a handful of lingering drug problems that still exist among the group. I sat in my office reading this, trying to understand what I could do to help. It is hard. It's challenging, stressful and every single night there is a point somewhere in the middle of the shift, when you want to walk off the line, because of the tax taken on your body – if it weren't for the brothers and sisters with whom we go into battle every night, it'd be a lot easier to make that walk.

He needed help and thankfully, sought it. He entered rehab and I didn't hear from him until his stint was over, a few months later. I had reached out to him in the time that had elapsed, hoping I could, perhaps, do something. When he responded to my message and explained where he'd been, a sense of relief took hold of me – it was one less casualty than I had anticipated based on our previous correspondence. We chatted, he referenced the original email from that night months ago, and of the horrifyingly dark place that he found himself in that night, but felt like rehab gave him a new lease on life. He had mended the relationship with his girlfriend, was given time with his children and was doing good work. I decided to write an article about how he had turned his life around and how the tragic ending that we've grown so familiar with in this industry doesn't have to exist so prevalently. We discussed what he had learned in the process and the article went viral – instantaneously. It was a message and a story that too many of us have experienced firsthand, or through the stories of those we care about. As he saw the positive response to his story, he responded and I could sense a smile on his face through the words he sent me.

"It's nice to see the response it's getting. It's nice to feel like my life is actually doing some good in the world for a change, thank you, Chris."

When he showed up that first day after reading the article and seeing the widespread impact of his story, he boasted into work how much it had meant to him that I used his story in such a powerful way.

Life went on per usual over the next few weeks and while I hadn't forgotten about or dismissed the gratifyingly peculiar relationship we had developed, life went on, as it always does, for both of us.

The following week, the cook working the station next to him, the man who had slugged out five hot summers in this beach town with him sent me an email.

He relapsed. He got into an argument with a co-worker. He hung himself.

It took hours to process such news. I was mad, confused, disappointed. I told my girlfriend and she just hugged me. I was bummed. This happens all the time. When I was waiting tables, during the early days of my life in restaurants and before I understood the dynamics of the kitchen, I walked into pre-shift one morning, hungover with a stained button-down from service the night before, an apron with unending wrinkles, and was blasted the news that a sweet girl that everyone in the building liked, had leaped to her death the night before. It was an investigation and details were fuzzy, but one thing that wasn't fuzzy was the fact that she was dead, had been using a variety of drugs, and had chosen to take her own life. Half a decade later, on a beautiful spring day during my early days of managing restaurants, I learned that my barback the night before had left work and had been smoking weed, sneaking drinks on the clock, or maybe both. He wrapped his truck around a telephone pole. He was twenty-two years old.

These types of stories can start to make you cold and hard and cynical, however, for me, after processing the most recent news of the cook's relapse, I knew I had to do something. So, I started writing this book.

I began asking questions like, "what does success look like?," and "how do you get there?" I certainly didn't have all of the answers, but perhaps I was further along the way road to it than some of my cohorts. I decided that the answer and a compelling one would be understanding those chefs and industry professionals that have made it – who have created success in their careers, but more importantly, in their lives as a whole. I wanted it just as much for other people, as I did for myself. I hadn't made it, at least the way I had envisioned and it made me mad to think about. I felt like I'd done everything right, but if I had, what was missing? What was I doing wrong? I was essentially broke and the restaurant world, while having given me a great deal of joy and gratification, had, in other ways, failed me and many of the people around me.

We all want to be able to do the work that lights us up, inspires us and is in sync with our passions, but it doesn't mean much if we jump into that work, and realize it's not sustainable – physically, psychologically, financially and relationally. There are a lot of things standing in the way of chefs and kitchen workers creating a successful career for themselves, but there are just as many beautiful reasons to fight through those challenges, in order to find fulfillment through a life in the kitchen, and that's what the stories in this book are all about. A beacon to the lighthouse of our careers that can help guide the way and show each of us that success in this or any industry is out there – you just have to show up and be willing to fight for it, every single day.

CHRIS HILL

"To the person who does not know where he wants to go there is no favorable wind."
SENECA

WHEREVER YOU'RE GOING, THERE YOU'll END UP

When I started off down this path at 19 and fell in love with the romantic, glamorized ideals of cooking, I kind of realized that it had been a part of me for as long as I could remember. Growing up in Atlanta, my siblings and I would gather around the breakfast table during the months of summer vacation. Both of my parents worked, in order to provide us four kids with everything we needed, so we'd find ourselves as youngsters having to fend for ourselves. Sure, a bowl of cereal worked just fine and I certainly ate my fair share of Quaker Oat creamed fruit oatmeal, but a lot more fun than that was making an interactive experience out of it. We would huddle around the kitchen, with pen and paper in hand, and create menus for ourselves. Taking turns cooking, we would serve each other a meal from the nominally listed price on the menu for items like French toast, egg-in-the-hole, toast with cheesy scrambled eggs and, if it was getting later in the morning, perhaps a grilled cheese and Campbell's tomato soup combo. Back in those days the cost of an item probably equaled the cost of making someone else's bed. It was never about the cost though, but rather the enjoyment of taking care of each other.

When I took my first restaurant job at the Atlanta Fish Market, I got the same adrenaline rush, as those days from my youth, the only difference was that that money actually meant something and the entire work process was like magic for me. Learning about all of the incredible seafood that came in the back door of that restaurant was almost incomprehensible to me. Nearly all of the fish that arrived on that back dock, aside from Alaskan Halibut, Chilean Sea Bass and Copper River Salmon, came from the east coast and was swimming in the Atlantic Ocean a few days prior to being cooked and served in one of the extravagant houses in Buckhead – no wonder it rang up in the computer as twenty five dollars a pound.

While there, I learned how to clean soft shell crabs by snipping off their eyes and apron, as well as the gills that were tucked under their bodies. It seemed strange, until trying one, that anyone in their right mind would think to crack open an oyster shell and marvel at the deliciousness of the slimy mollusk hiding inside, but once I did, my life was changed. I learned about the minute differences in various oysters; the bowl-like, sweetish Kumamoto and their history, versus the Bluepoints, Malpeques, Appalachicolas and the vastly different, though seemingly most familiar in shape, European Flats. I ventured into steaming and boiling seafood, which included everything from pisser clams to littlenecks, lobsters and, of course, shrimp, that was dropped into a seasoned pot of water that still, to this day, is the biggest piece of equipment I've seen in a kitchen. Here is where I learned that the "Old Bay" was the Chesapeake Bay and even after spending half a decade in Virginia, Old Bay will always remind me of boiling shrimp in the fish market. Jose, our fish monger, taught me how to break down fish by scaling it and then slicing vertically down the flesh of the fish, as close to the skeletal base as possible and then how to work your way up towards the collar, as well as the flesh towards the tail. He demonstrated with precision, as if he was performing surgery on someone. He taught me how to tweeze my way down a detached side of fish, until all the pin bones were extracted, and the first time he let me try to peel a fish's skin from the flesh, I sliced my index finger to the point where I should have had a stitch or two, but I didn't want to get Jose in trouble and I didn't want to lose my opportunity to learn more about this whole new world of which I had become so incredibly fascinated. I was his little gringo kitchen project and since I could speak Spanish, the jokes we could tell about the other, crazy white guys working in the market with me, always seemed to make his day.

I got a lot of cuts that summer. Yes, some were self-inflicted, while others resulted from the surprisingly sharp shells of U-10 shrimp or perhaps from the claws of a bright red lobster that somehow escaped the ever-so-important process of being rubber-banded. I also spent a lot of money on shoes, and clothes in general that summer. For an entire three months, I was unbearable to be around. The stench of my clothes and shoes was nauseating. Still living with my parents at the time, I returned home from work on day one and was forcefully told to leave my shoes on the porch outside. At the market, the fish sits in oversized buss tubs chock-full of ice in the walk-in cooler, which over time melts, creating a more-than-moist ground on which you find yourself working throughout the day. It's not just ice though, it's dead fish juice, of sorts, and it took no more than a handful of days to ruin my first pair of shoes that stunk like a dumpster in the Red Lobster parking lot.

The smell from that summer I will take with me for as long as I live, as it was then that I knew in my head, that I was supposed to dedicate my life's work to restaurants. Unfortunately, I didn't quite realize it at the time, and found myself floating through college while working in restaurants, primarily front of the house, however, I was always the member of the wait staff hanging out in the kitchen, bouncing ideas off of the various cooks, hoping to earn their respect and be one of the guys.

Upon finishing college with a double major in English and Spanish from the University of Alabama, I had zero vision for my life. I hadn't the slightest clue. I had no real value to bring to the marketplace that could utilize my college education. No one cared if I had read nearly every Shakespeare work out there, or if I could speak almost fluent Spanish. So, I went back to school in Tuscaloosa, Alabama, after a few years of meandering around, waiting tables, obtaining a real estate license that I never put to use and interviewing with business companies that were doing work that I had never heard of. I decided to go back to school, so I obtained my Master's in Marketing. I felt like this is what I was supposed to do. This is what all my friends were doing. This is what my dad did. This is what was going to get me a high-paying job making good money, so that I could find a girl and then buy a house and have kids. This is what everyone around me was doing and I was certainly pushed in that direction as well, quite unmaliciously. So, I finished grad school, got the decent paying job in the business world, but still didn't have any sort of vision for my life. I had enough trouble looking past Friday's happy hour, so trying to have an over-arching view of what I wanted for my life wasn't even something that I could comprehend. This bothered me and I decided to make a change. I quit, while the ink on my diploma was probably still drying. What now? Restaurants – something I should have done a long time ago. For the first time in my life, I did what felt right to me. Perhaps this would start to lead me down the path I think might be out there waiting for me.

This is when I started to understand what it meant to have a vision and the importance of actually having one. Up until this point I had been meandering through life, with no real direction or understanding of what I wanted to do with my life. To be perfectly honest, I think our educational system, especially here in the United States, fails us miserably. At the age of eighteen, when we finish high school and have to decide on heading off to college, hopping into the workforce or perhaps joining the military, most of us don't have the slightest clue what we might be interested in doing with our lives. So, I, like so many others found out the hard way, having to bounce around until something finally stuck with me and when it did, boy did it stick. It's all I could think about. However, I still didn't know the importance of creating a vision for myself. Sure, I've always been a hard worker and have always committed myself to being better than I was the day before, but why? What was the point? I didn't have an end goal in mind. Over and over again through these conversations, the idea of having a vision is one that has shown its face every single time. Brandon Chrostowski, the chef and owner of Edwin's Restaurant in Cleveland, is a great example of this. In the early days, however, his lack of vision almost ruined his life.

Brandon Chrostowski was born in and spent the early years of his life in Detroit. This was during the 80s and 90s before the giant collapse, but was instead right in the midst of its demise. His mother decided to move their family to the suburbs after the continued violence that had seeped into the nearly every nook and cranny of the city. Even in the suburbs, he found himself in close proximity to the street scene and finally, the life that Detroit had come to be known by caught up to him. The late high school years of dealing dope found him behind the wheel with flashing lights reflecting off of the mirror, and sirens bellowing through the foggy air off the lake. What happened next, he didn't seem to want to describe to me in much detail, but resulted in Chrostowski being arrested for evading the police. At nineteen he found himself behind bars and staring a ten-year prison sentence dead in the eyes.

Sitting behind bars, wondering what the fate for the future might hold, his vision for it was undoubtedly blurry, at the very least. There was no path for him and where his life might lead, however, the judge showed mercy and he was let out on probation. Brandon, saved by grace, was given another chance, another opportunity to make something of his life. He immediately began working with a local chef in the Detroit area who was classically trained and took him under his wing. The next year he enrolled in culinary school at The Culinary Institute of America.

After graduating from culinary school, he was able to work his way into the best kitchens in the world; Lucas Carton, a three Michelin Star restaurant in Paris, Le Cirque in New York, La Bernadin and others. While working in Chicago for Charlie

Trotter, at the height of his career, Brandon decided it would soon be time to act on something incredibly close to his heart. Never having felt very far-removed from the gavel and the painful past that could have turned into a devastating future, Brandon created a business plan and, a few years later, via a fundraiser, was about to raise half of a million dollars and would soon be opening up the first French inspired restaurant that would also serve as a culinary institute for recently released state prisoners. Chrostowski was given a second chance to make something of his life and felt indebted to those who weren't given that same opportunity. Before the restaurant actually opened, Brandon volunteered his time at the local prison just outside of Cleveland where he provided the same types of training and tools for inmates who weren't quite eligible for that second chance out in the real world.

Across the United States there are millions of housed prisoners who will earn the right to contribute to society outside of the barbed wire confines of a jail cell, but sadly, the recidivism rate is too high. Within three years, nearly two-thirds of all inmates are re-arrested and are back into the judicial system. It's clear that there isn't a fluid system that helps released prisoners in re-adjusting to life outside prison walls and Brandon saw this, not just as an adult, but as a boy growing up in the metro Detroit area. So, Edwin's came to be and was up and running in 2007. Every single employee in the restaurant has a recent criminal past, and the goal was to provide them with the tools and skills to not just work in a restaurant, but to actually excel and become a leader in one.

His mission is clear, and while he feels it will take more than just his lifetime, he truly feels that Edwin's can become the best culinary school in the country and little-by-little change the way we look at giving people a second chance.

"At first, no one knew what Edwin's was about, people just came in for the good food. I knew that if we offered a dynamic product, people would come, and they have. But, what was so exciting to see was that diners came in, not

to necessarily support the cause, but because they wanted one of the best experiences in Cleveland. It just goes to show anyone with the right tools can thrive, we just have to give them those tools and a second chance, just like I was given nearly twenty years ago."

His vision, which stemmed from his own internal childhood demons, was a fifteen-year dream in the making. He sat with the idea in his back pocket as he worked his way up through the best restaurants around until he knew it was time to strike. As he told me, "the mission drives the bus," and the mission first took shape as the restaurant. Since the opening days, Edwin's has expanded to provide classrooms, dorms and a host of instructors and mentors to help walk the recently released prisoners through day-to-day life in the real world.

"We start a different class every two months that lasts six months. Every single student works their way through the restaurant learning the different facets of restaurant operations. We provide housing for them during the program, and a five hundred dollar a month stipend. The next piece of the vision is an on-site gym, bakery, butcher shop and test kitchen. We are doing great things, but there is always one more thing and a different project to tackle. Of all the students that make their way through the six month program, we've had zero people return to prison. That's a pretty damn good track record. However, at the same time, half of all enrolled students drop out during the first three weeks. We work them hard, we put you through the ringer to make sure that you're willing to do the work necessary to contribute to our success, but for those that do make it through those challenging first several weeks, only 10 percent drop out, which is pretty incredible."

Brandon's commitment to his vision is so incredibly clear, in fact, he still heads down to the prison near Cleveland every Saturday and trains the inmates for life in the real world and has created a series of training videos that are now shown in prisons throughout the country. He spends a lot of time committed to this vision, and while he makes a decent salary, it's not one that represents the work he puts in every single day. He knowingly takes a pay cut, realizing that whatever additional pay that could come to him can now instead go into hiring one or two more people that will just help grow the business. It's not about him, it never has and it never will be – it's about the vision.

"For the longest time, I was convinced I'd never get married, because for me, the vision I had for Edwin's was so connected to who I was, that I knew I'd be making incredible sacrifices in order to see it through to success. I never thought I'd find a woman that would want to wait around for this dream to come to reality, but I was lucky and found one. She knows the commitment to Edwin's is the most important thing to me – it's what drives me, motivates me and inspires me to get out of the bed in the morning, knowing that big or small, I'm making a contribution to the whole."

I was blown away with Brandon and hearing his story. His vision is so incredibly crystal clear and in a way that I couldn't even comprehend. In talking, his nonchalance almost struck me as odd – he's been featured in magazines and newspapers all over the country and in 2015 was awarded the title of a CNN Hero. At the same time, he realizes there's always a bigger battle to fight than any he's previously tackled.

"I'm where I am today, because someone took a chance on me, because I was willing to work hard, and because of the fact that I had a vision for my life and what I felt compelled to do with it."

Well done, Brandon.

The problem I discovered with having a vision and putting it into practice is the fact that, along the way, it doesn't seem like you're getting anywhere. It's like running a marathon and asking "how much farther," after only completing the first mile. Edwin's is proof that having a clear vision of what you want to get out of your life is key in actually getting what it is that you want. At the same time, through his own life, and by successfully mentoring hundreds of students in and out of prison, we see that it is possible to start over in life, to take your life down a different path, and find a new direction to turn toward wherever you might be in life's journey, but it takes showing up to work every day with a willingness to learn today, in order to put oneself in a better position for tomorrow.

You have to know where you're going before you can start heading in the right direction. This whole idea of having a vision also reminds me of Chef Thomas Keller, perhaps the most heralded chef in the world over the last twenty years. He didn't go to culinary school, but had the opportunity to work his way up through the chain of command as a teenager in South Florida. He then bounced around in Europe, northern New York and then eventually opened Rakel in the City, in December, 1986. The first couple of years were gangbusters, Keller and his crew were doing the best food in town, but then the economy crashed and the lavish Wall Street bills weren't coming in as regularly as business all over the country tightened. Things got grim, which is when Keller and his business partner had a decision to make. They could either decide to lower the menu prices and make the food a bit more approachable which would, hopefully, get more customers in the doors and more sales running through the system. Or, they could close up shop and try to start over somewhere else, or perhaps at a different time. The decision for Keller was easy – they closed up shop. Keller had a clear vision for the type of food he wanted to do and he knew how much his customers appreciated the work he was doing, even if they couldn't afford it in the same way that they could a year or two prior.

Keller decided to move to California where he consulted a bit, until the timing was right. In 1994, deep in credit card debt and having to beg, borrow and steal from just about anyone he could get it from, The French Laundry opened and the rest is history, as they've won just about every industry award imaginable.

To create this kind of success obviously took a number of things, but it certainly took the commitment to one's vision, to see things through when life put hurdles in the way, but it also takes being intentional every single day. It's showing up to be the very best you can every single day. In his TEDx talk, Thomas Keller discusses interviewing young cooks who are looking to join The French Laundry team and explains how the conversation often goes.

"I ask a young culinarian, 'Why do you want to work here? Why do you want to cook?'"

"Chef, I can't tell you about how passionate I am about what I do!"

"Interesting, passion…I'm passionate as well. I'm passionate about the first Asparagus I see, the first baby Spring Lamb that comes in the back door. Yes, I'm really passionate about that, but after a week or two, what happens? My passion kind of subsides, it goes down a little bit, because I've been experiencing it for a couple of weeks – I'm kind of over it, but I still have an amazing asparagus that's coming in the door and I still have amazing Spring Lamb. What is it that's important to me in recognizing in that individual that he should be working in our restaurant? Or what is it in me that continues to drive me? It's desire. Desire. Desire trumps passion every time. It's nice to be passionate and passion's going to help move that desire higher, but when that passion isn't there, what do you need? You need desire…that strong sense of desire."

I couldn't agree more with Keller's approach. It's kind of like relationships, school or really anything in which we invest our time, desire is the key. Passion, as Keller notes, comes and goes and if we are continually reliant on it, we'll inevitably lose sight of our vision, because every now and then it will go away. Instead, it's that desire to get out of bed every morning and invest everything we have in the vision we have for ourselves – career, family and life as a while – that's what keeps us moving in the right direction. Every morning, we have a choice to connect with that vision and enlist our desire by improving ourselves and doing the best we possibly can, or we can go through the motions, much like I did when I sat behind a desk all day. When young, inexperienced cooks come to me asking for advice that will help put them on the right track, I always offer a few simple pieces of advice, but one in particular: be curious, and find something new to learn every single day, because if you intentionally find something new to learn every single day, even if it's something very minor, after an entire year, five years or ten, you're going to have a vast amount of knowledge that you otherwise wouldn't have necessarily acquired. It takes showing up with that desire and end goal in mind every single day. Over time, it's those today's and tomorrow's that add up to the sum total of one's life.

I always loved hearing the story of Jim Carrey, the incredibly talented actor who, in the late 1980s, had nothing but a vision. He'd drive down to Mulholland Drive at night and sit on the crest of land overlooking Los Angeles and just visualize the things that he knew were out there for him. He knew success was out there for him, if he just kept working hard and recommitted himself to the vision every single day. A few years later, in 1992, he wrote himself a check for ten million dollars for "acting services rendered" and dated it Thanksgiving Day, 1995. He kept that check tucked into his wallet and carried it around with him everywhere, until one day, right before that Thanksgiving in '95, he got a phone call from his agent. He'd been cast in Dumb and Dumber as a lead role. That movie made him just over ten million dollars, and the rest is history.

The question I'll leave you with here is this:

What are you doing today that serves the greater vision you have for your life?

Once you can answer that without batting an eye, that's when I think you're really on to something.

"Your work is going to fill a large part of your life and the only way to be truly satisfied is to do what you believe is great work. The only way to do great work is to love what you do."

STEVE JOBS

CHRIS HILL

CONNECTING WITH THE WORK

Having just finished earning my second degree from the
University of Alabama, I was so excited to jump right into
corporate America. Honestly, the only reason why I decided to
go back in the first place is because, as a freshmen and having to
decide what my major would be, I had a conversation with my
father and he suggested I aim for a well-rounded liberal arts
education, instead of focusing on business out of the gates – that
left me with a bunch of time and dollars spent on an education
that wouldn't translate into a job in the real word. All my friends
studied finance, real estate and accounting, while I was actually
taking classes that I really enjoyed. I obtained a double major in
English and Spanish, but again, there I was as a twenty-two year
old fresh out of college without the slightest clue of what I
wanted to do with my life. Back then, if it were up to me, I would
have gone into teaching English or Spanish so that I'd have
plenty of leisure time to focus on getting the novel I had been
writing completed. But I didn't have the best grades, I've never
been a grammar Nazi, and I wasn't really fluent enough in
Spanish to teach other people how to speak it, especially middle-
or high school-aged kids. So, I got a job waiting tables until I
could find a real job. All of my friends were utilizing their more
attractive degrees and were making pretty decent money out of
the gates and I couldn't have been more jealous. In fact, my
college girlfriend and I moved to Atlanta after our graduation and
my father was able to link her up with a solid entry-level interior
design job. I had job interviews with certain businesses similar to
the ones that my buddies were employed by, but I didn't have the

43

slightest context of business, so I bombed every single one. I did, however, get a pretty decent job at a restaurant waiting tables here in Atlanta. I was making two hundred bucks a night as a waiter at Hal's on Old Ivy, an Atlanta institution, and to this day I'm convinced they have the best steak in town. All of the waiters there were in their forties, fifties or even sixties, while I was barely in my twenties, making the same good money as them. I didn't belong, though. These were career servers, actual professionals who took tremendous pride in the connections that they were able to create with their customers, so I found myself mingling and hanging out with the Mexican busboys most of the time. I could speak their language and we were roughly the same age, so we'd joke back and forth throughout the shift, developing relationships that seemed to make more sense than my fellow pedigreed servers who could have all been my father.

I spent way too much money that year. Every night we'd get out of work and I'd buy the guys a round of drinks or some shots at the bar across the street. Hal, the owner of the restaurant owned their building as well, so we got the family discount – this wasn't a good thing. I drank way too much, woke up feeling like shit and moreover, would find my pants lying on the ground, realizing I'd blown the better half of my tips from the night before. Though I loved being in the industry, I didn't see a clear path to making a career out of it and I felt that I was letting my father down every day that I wasn't moving my life in a better direction toward obtaining that ideal job in the business world that would allow me to buy the picket fence house and become a member of the local country club – the one where we spent our childhood summers. So, that's when I decided to head back to school. I studied my ass off, did really well on the GMAT and got into the masters of marketing program at the University of Alabama, while also earning a scholarship based on my test scores. For the first time in my "adult" life, I felt like there was some direction to my life. I enjoyed that year of grad school, got great grades, created some lifelong friendships and had a job in consulting lined up upon graduation.

CHRIS HILL

I started that job in consulting back home in Atlanta and was excited out of the gates. Hell, this was my first real job, so to speak, so I didn't have any sort of measuring stick with which to compare it. It worked, at least for a while and it paid my bills. Unfortunately, though, things changed. I realized how much I hated sitting at a desk all day staying busy with grunt work, as I was the most junior of employees in our small office. Soon, in between checking Facebook statuses and browsing for new bands to follow on Pandora, I'd find some work to do. I'd fill out brainless spreadsheets, update slide decks and do whatever else my boss had neglected and most likely needed in a matter of minutes. The consulting work could have been really fun. I had the opportunity to learn about Fortune 500 companies through research, but also through interacting with their C-suite level executives, while also getting to work with their advertising agency partners. The work I discovered was very superficial though, and theoretically, my boss would have been much better off hiring some cheap labor overseas who could just keep up with the busy work. I began despising the work. I couldn't stand it, so I started a catering company on the side to try to keep my sanity. As a result, I found myself really enjoying the chance to entertain people around food and drink again. I felt connected to the work and the people, which was such a welcomed relief from the miserable existence that I'd come to accept over the last year or so of my life. It wasn't enough though, and every night I would come home to the plush apartment that my sister and I shared and drink myself silly until the wee hours of the night. One or two in the morning would come around and the fear of having to wake up and do it all over again the following morning paralyzed me. So, after a year and a half of hating my life, I once again decided to start over, which is when I moved to Virginia to work with my cousin, where I would then open the restaurant a year or so later. What was it that made this decision so easy for me, when everyone in my life thought I had completely lost my mind?

It was the connection to the work. What does that mean though, exactly? Here's a good place to introduce you to Chef Frank Stitt.

Stitt was born in the early fifties and raised in Cullman, the Northeast part of Alabama, to a successful family of doctors. His grandfather was a general practitioner in the area from the time Frank was a boy and then his father followed in his footsteps, becoming the most successful surgeon in the area at the time. Coming from a bloodline of success, Stitt was introduced to quality food from a young age. During our conversations, he spoke of trips to New York City as a child and having the opportunity to dine at the finest establishments in the country like the Four Seasons restaurant on the Lower East Side. At the same time, Stitt's maternal grandparents were good salt-of-the-earth American farmers who gave him the appreciation for the ingredients he would be cooking with twenty years later. The close proximity of Stitt's relationship to the land opened his eyes to the possibility of the crop's harvest. However, as a teenager and eventual high school graduate, he, unlike most of us, wasn't quite sure what to do with it. Having grown up in small town Alabama, Frank wanted to get away, so he enrolled in Tufts University in Medford, Massachusetts, where he spent the first two years of his formal education before journeying westward, influenced by the inspiration of Jack Kerouac and company.

So, after two years, Frank had a candid conversation with his father that would lead to another conversation several years later. He enrolled at the University of California at Berkley and began studying philosophy under Dr. Hubert Dreyfus, a leading Existentialist philosopher of the time. Here, his ideology began to take shape. At the same time, he was offered a position at Chez Panisse, the leader of the farm-to-table movement here in the United States. He had the opportunity to work with the best farms and the best ingredients under the reigns of Alice Waters and with the genius of Jeremiah Tower, while also acquiring a formal education that would go on to lead the way that has navigated his career.

I spoke with Chef Tower who described his style of leadership as someone who puts his team first, knowing that their success is essential to the success of the overall mission of the team. Later

in the book, you wil[l]
renowned restauran[t]
Restaurant where, t[h]
Dominique Crenn v
under him, but was
walked in asking fo[r]
restaurants, nor a f[o]
leadership and ran
his restaurant succe

In addition to the l
experiences with th
to the finest qualit[y]
able to parlay his n
with how we, as h[u]
meaning through t......

the day who were leaps and bound[s]
counterparts. He bounced arou[nd]
back to Birmingham in '82 a[nd]
Grill and then a stream of
Bottega, Bottega Café
Birmingham to serv[e]
but did so with a
they were mak[ing]
cases of veg[etables]
then ship[ping]
backy[ard]
It

success in Birmingham and throughout the world, it's imperative
to understand how this strand of philosophy has shaped how he
shows up to the work every single day. Existentialism, like most
philosophies, is quite dense, but the gist of it is that there is no
inherent meaning in what happens in the world around us, and
that each of us has a free will to act in a way that can be based on
what we perceive to be right or wrong – this is how we create
meaning out of an otherwise chaotic existence. So, how does this
tie back in to cooking and understanding the culinary world?
Well, Frank Stitt was offered the beauty of the bounty in the
Alabama countryside, and then again a few years later in
California. The average person might just take for granted the
fact that there is all of this beautiful abundance, not digging
deeper into it, except for the fact that it's just there and able to
provide us with nourishment. Stitt feels the obligation to truly
connect with it in a way that can make the world a better place. It
started when he moved back to Birmingham after a stint in
France where he was able to learn under the tutelage of Richard
Olney, which was made possible through an introduction by
Alice Waters. This opportunity led to hands-on work with Olney,
Julia Child, Simone Beck and the various other Francophiles of

ahead of their American

d France and then found his way

d opened up Highlands Bar and

others over the next fifteen years –

nd Chez Fonfon. He was the first chef in

not just sweet potatoes or radishes or beets,

geographical origin. He showed his diners that

ng the most delicious meals in the city, not with

etables that had been picked several weeks prior and

ped across the country, but rather from their own

rd, a few miles away.

as his connectedness to the work and the ingredients that he'd grown up with and then fallen in love with in California and then again in France, that allowed for him to create this different understanding of food. He realized that it was morally and ethically the right thing to do, to support the local farms and purveyors. Aside from just cooking great French-inspired Southern food, he gave something the diners could latch onto, something that they could connect with, as well. This, however, would only be possible through first enlisting a staff of evangelists who could rally around the same mission. Through his excitement of seeing various purveyors walk into the restaurant with a package of wild foraged watercress or fresh-ripened berries from their seventy-acre farm in Shelby County, just north of Birmingham. As he states,

"When the staff sees my joy and my excitement over these wonderful ingredients that walk through our doors every day, it shows them that these aren't just ingredients on a plate or in the walk-in cooler, but rather that they are a part of everything around us. The more I can connect with them, the more that they can see the beauty inherent in all of it. When I bring my cooks and staff out to the farm and they see the hens roaming around, the bulbs planted for the summer harvest and all of the other elements that we take so much pride in out at the farm, they then realize that these are the same ingredients that we have the opportunity to cook with every day. This is what excites me, and they see that this wild foraged watercress is more than just a plant inside a plastic green bag. They see that a hen is more than just a

CHRIS HILL

protein to sear in the pan along with some fresh herbs, mirepoix and wine to make coq au vin – these are actually animals and plants and they are all around us and it gives us such a different perspective and opportunity to connect with it."

Wow, does this make a lot of sense. I feel that for us cooks, so many of us, at least in my generation, whether we've been to culinary school or not, are completely out of touch with the world around us as it relates to the food we bring to life every day. A chicken is more than a split chicken breast Cryovac-sealed in a plastic bag and a piece of fish is more than a ten pound case that's tossed off the back of the purveyor's truck. I've always understood this, but it really took going back to my childhood as a boy when I'd spend our summer vacations on the shores of Charleston's barrier islands (to fully hit the message home). We would wade in the shallow waters of the inlet separating Sullivan's Island and Isle of Palms casting out strings wrapped around a wooden spool made by my grandfather that had chicken necks fastened tight around them. We'd spend hours at a time out there, baking in the sun, catching the crabs that we'd then go on to boil and then pick clean, extracting the very little meat that was hidden underneath their hard shells and in their tight claws. While casting over and over again, I'd watch my grandfather find a spattering of bubbles surfacing from the damp sand where the water meets the beach and would watch him dig his hand several inches into the Carolina sand and find a handful of baby clamshells. He'd meticulously pick through them, extracting the barely visible, raw clam hidden within – he'd do this with just as much calculation as he would picking the crabs on the porch later that afternoon and for the first time in my life, I realized that food just wasn't in a box, picked up in the drive-thru or even what we were used to buying at the supermarket – it was all around us, there waiting to be discovered, if only we'd open our eyes to look around.

So, what has been Stitt's mission over the last thirty-three years since opening his first restaurant in a city that vastly under-appreciated what he chose to make his life's work? It's this idea

49

of connecting with everything around us and finding meaning through that. His mission, though, has extended far beyond the original goal of supporting local farms and creating the best food possible through that. He and his wife Pardis, whom he calls the real brains behind the operations, were founding members of the Southern Foodways Alliance, a nonprofit whose goal, per their website is to, "document, study, and explore the diverse food cultures of the changing American South. Our work sets a welcome table where all may consider our history and our future in a spirit of respect and reconciliation." The organization that is doing great things throughout the American South, of which Pardis is still on the board, isn't too different from the Slow Food Movement, which the Stitts were founding members of in the local Birmingham chapter. The Slow Food Movement focuses on understanding the impact that our food choices have on the world around us – the environment, the economy and our society as a whole. Thus, it's clear to see how one man's opportunity to work with the folks who started the farm-to-table movement in the United States began his quest to make his restaurant more than just about the food – it's about our society and the greater melting pot of our culture as a whole. Waters, Tower, Olney and the rest of the early influencers of Stitt's career helped shape what has been a movement throughout the Southeast. It was through connecting with these ideals that has allowed for him to grow and mature as both a restaurateur and a man.

His gracious nature gave me chills throughout our conversation and he was able to hammer home a concept that I continually preach, over and over, to myself and to those whose attention I've been fortunate enough to earn – it's more than food. It's about the relationships we have to the whole and our responsibility to act in a way that benefits the world around us, and in doing so, the rest kind of takes care of itself. As we were chatting, I alluded to the fact that he'd played such an important role in the career of Chef Chris Hastings, a James Beard Award winner in his own right (Hot and Hot Fish Club, Ovenbird), but he was quick to stop me in my tracks.

CHRIS HILL

"Chris worked with me for three years before heading to California where he refined his skills before coming back to work with me for three more years – that's when he opened his first restaurant. But there are also six or eight others here in Birmingham who've worked their way through our various restaurants that are doing incredible things. It's nice to know that I might have played some small role in the eventual success of these incredibly talented people."

I was floored. Chef Frank Stitt's fingerprints were all over the Birmingham dining scene, and whether the rest of the country knew it or not, he had put Birmingham on the map. I kept digging, trying to figure out what it was that was different about these other incredible chefs from those that might have had the technical skill, but just couldn't seem to create that same level of success for themselves. Stitt continued,

"Those that have worked under me or for me that have gone on to create success for themselves, they understand this. They understand that it's not just about them, but it's about truly connecting with other people and the world around us. The problem is, they don't teach us this in culinary school and the nature of where our industry is going with cutthroat cooking competitions everywhere distracts from it as well. It's about connecting to the work. That's what it's all about."

"There are always two choices. Two paths to take. One is easy. Its only reward is that it's easy."
ANONYMOUS

THE POWER OF A DECISION

After globetrotting throughout his early twenties post-graduation from the New England Culinary Institute in Vermont, Gavin Kaysen found himself working in Switzerland alongside the shores of Lake Geneva for a stint and then in London slaving away for the infamous chef, Marco Pierre White at his restaurant L'Escargot. After working eighteen-hour days for several years, he returned stateside and was given his first executive chef job at El Bizcocho in San Diego. At just 24 years old and perhaps having a bit of the ignorant arrogance of an up-and-coming hot shot, Kaysen started making some noise and, following his heart and intuition, wrote a letter to the respected and renowned chef, Daniel Boulud. The letter was his way of getting on the chef's radar, wanting to stage at the chef's namesake restaurant, Restaurant Daniel. Kaysen spent a week in one of New York's finest restaurants in 2005 and he did indeed end up on Boulud's radar. In 2007, Gavin represented the United States at the Bocuse d'Or in Lyon, France, something Chef Boulud has been heavily involved in. He took months of work off, in order to train for what are known as the culinary Olympics, and by the end of the competition found himself a quarter of a million dollars in debt. When the committee announced the protein to be used for the event, Bresse chicken, he had no choice but to move to France to train, because of the fact that the chicken wasn't able to be exported to the States. Each country has one participant representing them and they get a commis during the competition, as well, who serves as their assistant. This promising young cook naturally makes considerably less money based on where they are in their career, and Kaysen knew his commis couldn't afford to cover the cost of travel, a new roof over his head and everything else that goes along with uprooting one's life, so Gavin paid him out of his own pocket, adding to the pile of money that he'd already funneled into this dream.

This was America? How was there no funding for the competition? All the European countries had funding and support, why not the U.S.?

Following his disastrous fourteenth place finish in 2007, Kaysen vowed to help the United States make their way up to the podium. With the help and encouragement of creating a foundation by Paul Bocuse's son Jerome, along with Daniel Boulud, the idea for a foundation was in the works that would help fund the competition stateside. A reluctant Thomas Keller agreed to help after receiving a phone call from Chef Bocuse himself and in 2008 the foundation Ment'Or was founded to help support the American team that hadn't placed better than fifth since they began competing in 1987. The foundation's goal was to provide support, primarily financial, leading up to the competition that would allow for the U.S. to prepare more efficiently and, at the very least, there wouldn't be a burden on the participating chef to be the only individual making a significant financial contribution to the event.

Now, the foundation holds fundraisers and accepts donations, which has given the United States the tools and resources to make their way onto the podium. In '09, Timothy Hollingsworth placed 6th, and it looked like the foundation's support might actually be helping. Two years later, James Kent from Eleven Madison Park placed 10th, and then in 2013, Chef Richard Rosendale of The Greenbrier placed 7th overall. Kaysen looked at Chef Keller with disappointment after that respectable finish and said,

"I'm sick of this. I want to get on the podium."

In 2014, after much hard work and helping with putting the foundation together, Chef Kaysen was named the coach of the U.S. team and then later one day in late March of the same year, while training with the candidate for the following year, Phillip Tessier, at Thomas Keller's French Laundry, news broke – Kaysen was leaving Café Boulud and Manhattan. He wasn't just heading to Brooklyn or Long Island, but he was leaving New York City altogether and was heading home to Minneapolis, to set up shop there.

His decision to move to the Midwest and into a metro area that isn't particularly well known for their culinary scene was confusing to most. Why ever leave New York City, the mecca of the chef world in the modern age? As cooks and chefs we work off mise en place lists – a checklist of items worked on the day before that readies us for service the following day. The list is curated and the next morning it's there waiting for us. The mise en place list is based on a cook's station, thus the prep required for the following day, as well as that for the coming shift is dependent on what station a cook is working, and at the end of the day, the restaurant's menu. When designing a menu a chef considers the economy of the kitchen and in creating it, sets it up in a way that the load is equally distributed. Kaysen made menus for Boulud's three Café group of restaurants for nearly five years. Not only was this in New York City, but he oversaw the sister restaurants in Toronto and Palm Beach, and worked with the executive chefs of each location on the creation of their menus throughout the year. Though Kaysen had a tremendous amount of autonomy and was unquestionably seen as Boulud's right hand man, they still weren't his menus, per se. Sure, they had his fingerprint and thoughtfulness embedded throughout, but he still couldn't do things exactly as he would, his way – in a sense, until he was on his own, it would always be the Café Boulud way.

The decision to move his family a thousand or so miles west to the land of many lakes, a place that housed all of his childhood memories, made sense. He could do things his way and, more importantly, take his family with him to impact an entirely different community. When talking with him about the decision, Kaysen spoke of the gratification of leaving the Big City on his terms,

"Most people that leave New York City leave because they can't make the cut here. I proved over the eight years that I was there and working with Daniel that I was cut out for it and did great things. Now, I want to do the same great things with my family in, what I consider to be my home."

A two-year exit plan was put in place that would allow for, then chef de cuisine, Aaron Bludorn to step into the role that he was, for all intents and purposes, completely ready for – executive chef. This allowed Kaysen to work through his plans for relocation to Minneapolis. The decision, as Kaysen describes it, had a bigger impact than he could possibly have imagined.

"Chefs were saying, 'Oh, Gavin is coming home, we need to step our games up,' but underneath that is something a bit more nuanced. By them stepping their game up, whether it was for me or otherwise, plus me coming into town, raised the stakes for the entire region. No longer did a would-be chef have to move off to New York or one of a few other hot restaurant scenes – these cooks could stay home, get really good here and help change the dynamic along with me."

Success wasn't guaranteed and that voice in the back of his head reminded him that that was the case. Would the same cuisine work in Minneapolis? Would he be a flash in the pan? Then what happens?

Gavin states,

"Without risk I have no fear, without any fear – what's the point, because then I have no opportunity for success."

Chef Kaysen's restaurant, Spoon and Stable, opened in the fall of 2014 and Daniel Boulud stopped in during the buildout as it came to life to check on the man whose life he helped shape. Out of the gates they won Best New Restaurant by the James Beard Foundation, as well as (what did they win – best new restaurant?) Food & Wine and Bon Appétit Magazines.

Two years later Kaysen would be coaching Philip Tessier, the executive sous chef of the French Laundry. Gavin explained how, when Tessier learned of the opportunity to compete, a light bulb turned on in his head. Everything shifted. He had committed himself to the cause unlike anyone he'd ever seen before. His whole focus became the event that would give him and the U.S. contingency a chance at redemption two years later, in 2015. The goal was to reach the podium.

As I chatted with Tessier, the drive became clear, as he dove into what exactly he did to put himself in the best position to succeed.

He quit his job at the French Laundry for nine months in order to begin training. He stopped drinking for twenty-two months leading up to it, worked out doing CrossFit every morning, took French lessons, started applying better eating habits that would fill in his 145 pound frame, and embraced a mindset that wouldn't settle for anything less than everything he had – it resonated across all aspects of his life. The father of three children under the age of ten made the choice to dedicate his entire existence to realizing this dream of standing on the podium.

"You get five and a half hours and one shot at this. There is no second chance. I didn't want to get there and think, 'what if', or 'if I had only done this.' We did everything we could to prepare ourselves physically, mentally and even spiritually, because I knew I couldn't live with myself if the end of the competition came and we had to watch other competitors representing their countries, knowing I could have done something different or invested more."

You need to have this kind of alignment, because unlike Chopped or any other cooking competition on T.V., this is the real deal – a bunch of hungry, quite literally, Europeans pack themselves into an auditorium that holds thousands of people.

It's loud and it's hot and the competition is much like the dinner service of a busy restaurant, hours and hours of preparing, which will – in the end – hold the fate of a chef's place in the competition. Years of hard work boiled down to one intense and stressful afternoon, where there is no room for error. As a competitor, you don't stop moving for five and a half hours, so if you're out of shape or ill-prepared in any way, you're doomed. In fact, the American team made their way overseas with luggage and boxes worth of supplies, kitchen equipment and gadgets, but the entire shipment got stuck in customs on the way into France. What could have doomed their chances and killed any hope for changing the course of history, worked out in the nick of time.

In front of a raucous group of bellowing Europeans, the competition took place in the dreary, bone chilling latter part of January 2015. Getting an unfortunate draw, the U.S. team had to compete on day one of the two-day event, which is historically the less favorable of the two days. Competing alongside Canada and France, among others on that first day, the team knew they were in for a battle. Part of what each team is judged on is based on their ability to express the unique culture and culinary traditions of their home country, which has traditionally been quite challenging for the U.S. competitors, because of a certain lack of that very tradition and understanding of what American cuisine really is. Nevertheless, come day's end, a buzz was in the air that the United States team had out-performed their fellow competitors. Now, it was a waiting game, as they had to wait around for the heavy hitters of day two. After a long day of anxiously killing time, the day came to a close and it was time for the awards presentation.

Sweden received third place and tension in the room tightened as Chef Grant Achatz, the acclaimed American chef went on stage to announce second place. With the crowd of thousands now having turned into theater patrons and on pins and needles, deathly still with anticipation, two ladies snuck up next to the U.S. team, and before he could even announce, the team knew it – they did it, they made the podium.

"United States," he smiled with a bit of patriotism, and the entire team cheered, hugged and as Kaysen recalled, "all I could hear was Chef Keller yelling over and over, "I LOVE YOU GUYS, WE DID IT!"

Kaysen's decision to follow his heart and write that letter to Daniel Boulud in 2005 is what set the chain of events in place. That was the decision, and it wasn't an easy one, as he'd never worked with Daniel, but in doing so was given the opportunity to work under one of the best in the business. Then, Kaysen competed in the Bocuse d'Or himself – when he finished in a heartbreaking fourteenth place, he made another decision, by vowing to do everything he could to change the future for the American team. Shortly thereafter, the eight-year working relationship with Boulud deepened, the creation of Ment'or to fund the competition stateside, and the eventual invitation for Kaysen to partake in the competition again from Boulud himself – this time as a coach. We know how the story ends as this time around the team earned second place honors, having lost by only a fraction of a percentage point to Norway. The mission was accomplished. They made it onto the podium.

Sometimes it's the big decisions that change the direction and shape of our lives, while at other times, it's recommitting ourselves to that decision we once made long ago – our careers, our bodies, loved ones, our communities and whatever it is we choose to stand for. It starts as one decision, but over time, the impact of that one decision is inextricably linked to who we've become. The power is in one's ability to string together little affirmations for whatever that decision is, every single day, and this couldn't be more true than in understanding the level of commitment that Tessier exhibited day in and day out, in order to reach the goal that he and a whole host of others set out to achieve.

This idea of having a vision and then following one's heart makes a lot of sense, and always has to me, however, often we find ourselves following our heart, because something feels right – a job, a relationship, a new city to live in – but we don't actually have a clear vision of what that future might be, the sacrifices it will take to get there, and the overarching challenge that we are forced to grapple with if we do set out to create a life for ourselves versus unintentionally floating through life with the rest of the pack, becoming vulnerable and susceptible to the shifts and turns of life. This takes courage, though, and unless you have that strong vision for your life, it's pretty easy to give in, take the easy way out and listen to that voice in the back of your head saying, "maybe they're right."

When I went to grad school seven years ago, it was for the wrong reasons; it was to make the people around me happy – my family, my girlfriend, the community of people with whom I surrounded myself. I went, because, well, I had a double major in English and Spanish, and I would never get a decent job in the business world without it. If I would have listened to my heart, and the type of life and work I wanted for myself, I never would have gone. I realized the hard way, by feeling stuck at a job I wasn't happy with, while doing work that didn't matter to me. When I quit, I was able to dive head first and elbow-deep into what my heart was telling me and I haven't turned back since. It wasn't complicated. It just took taking a few steps back and listening to my heart. If I ever find myself in a rut and feeling uninspired, I ask myself one very simple question,

"What's my heart telling me?"

Whatever it is that I hear, I do that, every single time and I'm always happy that I did. Bad news though, even if you follow that inspired heart of yours, you'll find yourself unmotivated, if the work you're doing isn't "yours" and if it's not important to you. We do work to please our bosses, clients, and audiences, especially as artists, by creating things we think the mainstream will appreciate. Nothing is inherently wrong with any of this and there is certainly a time and place for it, but there is an unhealthy reason for why we've all been conditioned this way. We've been born and raised in a time and place where a nice paycheck and a fancy car have greater value than doing important work. So many of the choices we make every single day are made, consciously or not, in order to make the people around us happy. Sure, there are exceptions, but let's be realistic, doing meaningful work is great, but if it doesn't pay the bills, who cares? Well, you care, and so does author Neil Gaiman. He offered a poignant testament to this idea in a 2012 commencement address. He details writing a book that should have become a bestseller, but instead, the publishing house went under, the second print run never happened, and he never saw any royalties from it. In reflection, he said to the graduates,

"I'd do my best in the future not to write books just for the money. If you didn't get the money, then you didn't have anything, and if I did work that I was proud of and I didn't get the money – at least I'd have the work. Every now and then I forget that rule, and whenever I do, the universe kicks me, hard, and reminds me. I don't know that it's an issue for anybody but me, but it's true that nothing I ever did for the money was ever worth it—except as bitter experience."

"There are no shortcuts to any place worth going."
BEVERLY SILLS

BUCKLE UP

Bags packed, plans made and an extended trip overseas imminent, Viviani got news from his father of legal trouble that, without his help, would result in the family losing everything. With the liquidity of recently sold restaurants and nightclubs (5 and 2), Viviani used his hard-earned assets to take care of his family once again, as he'd been doing for years. He wasn't handed anything, but rather earned it every step of the way, starting out as an eleven year-old boy.

What the hell was I doing at eleven years old? Sports around the calendar year, sleepovers with friends, summer camps, and the list goes on. Nothing I did at that point in my life pointed to me having any sort of responsibility. The first time I made money was working as a camp counselor and then the following year, when the Olympics came to Atlanta in '96, the cycling competition ventured down the street of our childhood home on Putnam Drive and took the opportunity to make a few bucks by selling bottled water and Gatorade to the fans that had come out to watch their favorite cyclists in the scorching heat of July. We made a few bucks pacing up and down our neighborhood over the course of a few days, but not because we had to – we wanted to.

Fabio Viviani, on the other hand, was born into a hardworking family in Florence, but didn't have the same resources that we, fortunate American kids, had growing up. At six, Viviani was wearing a chest brace to counter the scoliosis that had developed from sleeping on a recliner instead of a bed. On food stamps and occupying a 300 square foot apartment with his parents and grandparents, there wasn't enough space nor money to provide for him, the way I've come to take for granted. His parents, honest and intent on providing for Fabio the best they could worked two full-time jobs each, still unable to make ends meet in a way that provided for their family. Beds backed into the dining room table, which backed into the kitchen where, if nothing else, there was an appreciation for good, rustic Italian food that, based on necessity, became the place where fresh Italian food was made and was utilized in a way that wasted nothing.

At eleven years old, Viviani's mother became ill. She could no longer work, all the while medical bills began to mount. The healthcare system couldn't sufficiently provide for them and the government assistance wasn't enough, so Fabio, who had already grown into more responsibility than I could have imagined at the time, was forced to get a job. But how? How does an eleven-year-old get paid to do a job that they probably don't know how to and most definitely aren't legally permitted to do. He walked into a bakery one day, explained the situation and before he was even a teenager, was working the graveyard shift making pies for the restaurant empire of Simone Mugnaini in Firenze. For the first week, Fabio showed up on his bike, which was stolen soon after, a casualty of living in the slums in any city around the world. Nevertheless, by working the shifts in the dead of the night, Viviani could make the money needed to float his family through the obstacles, while also staying out of trouble (for the restaurant as well), because no government agencies would be looking into child labor during those quiet nights in the bakery. He would work the nights, shower and change for school and head off to class through the afternoon hours, return home from school in time for a short nap and was back at work, committed to feeding and taking care of his family.

Those nights turned into days and at sixteen he became the sous chef of one of Mugnaini's other restaurants. Then, at 18, having seen the loyalty and hard work, Fabio was offered a share in the restaurant as a partner. So, after putting in seven long years of work he was in business for himself for the first time and wouldn't look back. In our conversation, Fabio spoke of how, by the time he had reached this age, he had already woken up on three different occasions to the beeping red lights and mellowed fluorescent bulbs of a hospital room, some two days after having being submitted there – exhaustion.

The closest thing I had known to medical exhaustion up until this point in my life was selling those ice cold bottles of water during the summer of '96, or perhaps having to run excess wind sprints during pre-season training for basketball – fortunately, they resulted in me making the varsity team – but never were the stakes very high. My family's livelihood was never on the line.

As a result, Fabio became a business owner at eighteen and didn't turn back. He's worked for himself, almost exclusively, ever since. Over the next decade, he helped grow the business started by Mugnaini and at twenty-seven found himself to be the co-owner of five restaurants, a farmhouse and two nightclubs in Florence. He'd made it. New ventures awaited him – America.

I can't imagine what it would be like to be a millionaire at twenty-seven. At that age, I was starting over, having just finished graduate school and my short stint in consulting. This is the point that I decided to leap into restaurants full-time. At the same age, Fabio Viviani, a native of Florence, Italy, decided to pack his bags and vacation for a good year or so on the other side of the Atlantic, in California. Years of hard work allowed him to create a nest egg of sorts that would allow for him to enjoy his time in the United States versus grinding away like he had been the last fifteen years of his life in Firenze.

Then, he got the call. His father had found his way into legal trouble. Everything he'd worked so hard for was gone. So, at 27, Fabio found himself once again broke, and this time in a country whose language he didn't speak. All he knew was that he'd done it before and he could do it again. It was the relentless work ethic that had gotten him to where he was and what he had planned on being an extended vacation that was long overdue became another chapter in his life that would be dedicated to nestling his nose right up to the grindstone. He didn't have any other choice.

Viviani moved to Ventura Country, California with no understanding of the English language, but he did have a commitment to busting his ass to go along with a skillset in the kitchen that proved to be quite valuable. At this point, he'd spent fifteen years in commercial kitchens, and was able to quickly work his way up the line, learn English and, in the process, learn Spanish as well (a close relative to Italian). He started making his mark – on American soil this time – and he did so starting from scratch.

One evening a couple came in looking to have their wedding catered at the restaurant at which Fabio was working. Overhearing the situation and a sobbing soon-to-be bride, he realized that the chef/owner had highballed the price to a point where this couple couldn't afford it. Fabio gently pulled them aside and offered to do it himself. He knew the recipes. He knew what the couple wanted. He knew he could make them happy, and he did. Soon after the dinner, the same couple was begging for him to come on Bravo's Top Chef. They knew the producers and they knew he could make a name for himself.

Four years after offering to prepare that fateful wedding dinner for that disappointed couple, Fabio agreed to be on the show for their fifth season. He didn't chase the shiny luxuries of TV life. Hell, back in Italy, the only folks that ended up on TV were news anchors, celebrities and criminals – he wasn't any of those. The idea of cooking on TV didn't make sense at first, plus his English was still sub-par. After declining to participate on each of the show's first four seasons, Fabio gave Bravo the nod. He was ready. At this point, he'd opened his own restaurant, Cafe Firenze in Moorpark, his English was better and he was at the point financially, where he could afford to take the risk, as he couldn't get fired and he wouldn't have to worry about where his next paycheck might come from. Now, he was writing the paychecks.

Top Chef opened the doors to success, perhaps just a bit wider for Fabio Viviani – he'd already made it, twice. He created success back home in Italy, and again just four years into his stint living in the States after having to start over. It was the work ethic he developed at a young age that carried over into his formative, then early adult years that allowed for him to compete with the best chefs in the country, in what was arguably Top Chef's most competitive season. He didn't win, but finished in fourth place after not creating a compelling enough version of the American classic, the hamburger However, he did take home, in a landslide, the "Top Chef Fan Favorite." This opened the doors to success a bit farther and Fabio took advantage of it, pushing those proverbial doors wide open. He grew into the personality we've grown to adore throughout the U.S., now owns ten restaurants, has published three cookbooks, owns a wine label, is known for product endorsements as well as over one hundred TV appearances a year, plus inspires audiences around the country through both his newly formed Know How Leadership Academy, as well as by sharing his story in keynote presentations. He is an inspiring guy, with an inspiring message. As we were talking and as our time came to a close, I asked him,

"Fabio, what do you think it is that holds most people back from creating the type of success they are hoping to achieve in their life and in their career?"

Without hesitation, he chimed in.

"Excuses. Everyone has an excuse. You see them get out of work on the weekend and they go out to the bar or are celebrating on vacation – what are you celebrating? You haven't created the success you want for your life yet! And the problem with America is not that people dream too big and miss, it's that they dream too small and hit! I mean, how did we get to the point where the goal in this country is to make fifty thousand dollars a year with four weeks of paid vacation and enough money to buy a Toyota?

So you have a forty hour a week job? Great, you might as well have a hobby. If you want to be successful, you have to work hard every single day, plus work really hard on making yourself better so that you are always becoming more valuable to the people with whom you work, otherwise, there will always be someone who can do the same work as you, but chances are, they will either work just a little bit harder than you or will be just a little bit cheaper than you. You think I got to this point in my life and career by working forty hours a week? Hell no, and the only people that judge me are the ones who don't have what they want and haven't created the same success in their lives, because they aren't willing to put into the work.

Me? I grew up on food stamps in the slums of Italy, I've been working since I was eleven years old, had earned a million and lost a million by the time I was twenty-seven. Then, I moved to a country where I didn't speak the language, with no money. So the question I want to ask people is this,

"WHAT'S YOUR EXCUSE?"

We aren't all blessed with the same talent, the same IQ, or cash in the bank account starting out, but the one thing each of us has in common is the number of hours in the day. The rest of it, none of us can control, so in a sense, it's a level playing field, or at least it helps to look at it that way. The question is, how are you going to choose to spend those days? The guy or girl who is willing to work harder than anyone else trumps the one with talent every day of the week. If you put two individuals side by side with identical skills, talent and experience, the playing field is leveled, at least hypothetically. Who is going to be the better cook, artist, athlete or businessman? That's easy – it's the one who is willing to work harder.

We live in a society obsessed with the overnight success, but let me break it to you – it doesn't exist – it never has and it never will. Anyone can buy a lottery ticket and by luck of the draw land a huge sum of money, but there is a reason why those individuals almost always lose it all. Sure, it has to do with ignorance as it relates to handling money, but I firmly believe that no one would call those individuals successful, whether they squander it or not, because they didn't work for it, they don't appreciate it.

My body hurts. Badly. Everywhere, and that includes my head. My eyes don't want to open, and they don't really have to yet, at least I don't think they do. The humming of lawn mowers blares in the background, and my thoughts are that it is still early. Yesterday was another 18-hour day, and I keep thinking that pretty soon this will all catch up to me. Maybe it will at some point, but it can't yet, I haven't gotten there yet. I haven't made it, damnit.

I have since crawled out of bed and into my car and headed to work for the monthly bar clean. It is over now and I sit at the bar and reflect on the past week with a mimosa, my laptop, and golf whispering in the background behind me. Thank god the restaurant is closed on Sundays.

The first time my parents came into town to visit me at the restaurant (that I then owned) was exciting, however, emotional. I was incredibly proud to show them my first restaurant. Several years prior I took this leap of faith and I was eager to prove to them that I was on my way. I cooked them lunch as they wandered around the restaurant inspecting the art, perusing the menu and talking about the restaurant that was partly mine. I constructed a couple sandwiches for them made of fig-glazed pork tenderloin, our house roasted tomatoes, smoked Gouda cheese and a super savory herb aioli. I nestled them onto separate plates, filled the dead space with parmesan-dusted potato chips, and walked over to hand them their lunch, while telling the guys on the line that I'd be back in a few minutes. I explained exactly what they were going to be eating, and grabbed a seat next to Cheryl, my adoring and ever-gracious stepmom. They ate, and we caught up on life – how things were going at home, how I was liking life in Virginia. The whole time they seemed to be smiling at what I had made for them. It is hard to describe the emotion that shot through me on that first day my parents came into the restaurant. If nothing else, it shows me that I am doing the right thing with my life, and that moving up there, while risky and uncertain, proved to be paying off. Even the long hours of burning the candle at both ends now somehow seemed worth it, like I made it. I wish I could rest now, knowing that my parents were proud of the steps I had been taking toward the future, but I couldn't and can't rest, because this is only the beginning. Especially in restaurants, there is always, always, always something to do. You can always make the door to the reach-in cooler a bit shinier, clean the front-of-the-house just a bit more and crunch the numbers, as it relates to food costs, in order to save the restaurant a few extra bucks here and there – over time, that can really add up.

We made it through a busy lunch and I was able to sneak out before the grunt work of breaking down the shift came into play. I've always hated darting off the line for a meeting, a phone call or anything some might deem more important, however, for the first time in a long time (definitely since we'd opened), there was actually something more important to attend to. The rest of the day I showed my parents around town. We drove the streets of the beach community where they both grew up, though none of it seemed to strike them as familiar. All of the nostalgia of their childhoods had been replaced with over-commercialized streets lined with tourist-ridden sidewalks, shops and restaurants. We had dinner and drinks and enjoyed each other's company, which came all too brief, when we hugged at the end of the night.

The next morning as I was putting the final touches on a delicious mushroom bisque for lunch service, Cheryl wandered up to the door. She and my dad were on their way to the airport, and wanted to say goodbye one last time. I hugged her, as my dad smiled from the rental car in front of me, and we embraced for a couple of moments. I told my line cook Ron to keep half an eye on the soup, and to power-off the grinder that was pulverizing some mushrooms that I'd recently dried into a powder. That would serve as the garnish to the soup. I scampered out to bid farewell to my father who was anxiously honking in the loading zone across the street and handed Cheryl a to-go bowl of the soup that was finishing up. It was close enough. I handed it to her, as I thought about our wonderful time yesterday, what exactly it meant that they came to see me, and how this emotion that was written all over me could easily be translated into the future. My dad beckoned, hurriedly began pulling out of the parking spot, in the way that he's done since I was a child (always stressed about getting to the next place on time) and I offered my thanks for them stopping in. I handed her that cup of soup, blew them a kiss, and wandered back inside to where the grinder was still powdering my mushrooms and where my station was awaiting me in the hot kitchen that had become my home over the last few years. We got busy over the next couple of hours, really busy, like always, and it wasn't until after the lunch rush that I got the chance to check my phone. There was a message from my parents,

"Soup was delicious, kiddo."

All along I knew this was the right move, I just needed this to help realize that. Little did I know that this was only the beginning, not just of my successes, but more importantly, of the actual work that I'd have to put in to create this success. Over the next three and a half years I spent nearly sixteen hours a day in that kitchen. Every chance I got, I was flipping through my *Flavor Bible* looking for new ingredients to work with. Often, I'd wander over to the store looking for new ingredients with which I could work. Many nights, long after the restaurant had closed for the day, I'd sit at the bar at the restaurant playing around with recipes on my legal pad which I would then work on long enough until they worked. At that point I could write them down and share them with my staff for the following day. For years I spent more time at work putting in those infamous 10,000 hours, in order to get better at the craft I'd chosen for myself. Talent we are born with, to varying degrees, but talent without skill will only take you so far. It's the combination of some degree of talent, along with hard work that allows us to excel at our craft. Unlike a lot of late twenty-something young men, I didn't jump into restaurants full-time at nineteen, twenty-two or twenty-five. I was twenty-seven when I officially jumped in full time and I was making up for lost time. I didn't have the skills that I knew I'd need to develop if I wanted to be a successful chef. I've never been the best cook – not the most creative, organized and certainly not the best trained – but I will never be outworked. I've always loved the Will Smith quote from some interview he gave several years back when he refers to his work ethic,

"The only thing that I see that is distinctly different about me is I'm not afraid to die on a treadmill. You might have more talent than me, you might be smarter than me, but if we get on the treadmill together – there's one of two things that are going to happen: you're getting off first, or I'm going to die! It's really that simple."

Treadmill, kitchen, wherever it is, one thing is for damn sure – I will not be outworked. Of all the things that are outside of my control, my ability to show up and work hard every single day – that isn't one of them. It's not dependent on my talent. It's not dependent on how much money is in my bank account, how good looking I am or how well I did in school. My work ethic has nothing to do with you and it has nothing to do with my past or anything else, aside from my will to put in the work. Right this second, the only thing standing in the way of where I am right now and where I want to be is the work that I've already committed myself to doing.

Now, what about you? Are you putting in the work? If not, I'll go back to the question Fabio Viviani likes to ask,

"WHAT'S YOUR EXCUSE?"

CHRIS HILL

"The reason that art is valuable is precisely why I can't tell you how to do it. If there were a map, there'd be no art, because art is the act of navigating without a map. Don't you hate it? I love that there's no map."

SETH GODIN

CHRIS HILL

WRESTLING WITH THE TENSION

Man, oh man, was it scary wrangling up the nerve to try and have the conversation with my dad that would change the course of my life. Would I be letting him down? He had worked so hard to provide every opportunity for me to succeed, and I felt that, by leaving that job in the corporate America, I'd be somehow letting him down. At first maybe I did, however, at the same time, I think he understood that I needed to take a leap of faith, in order to figure out what would be best for myself in the long run. Unfortunately, the short- and long-run perspectives of our lives are vastly different. Almost always, as we are trying to find our way to success and happiness, we discourage ourselves – that inner voice inside our head starts questioning things and tries talking us out of the things that we really need to figure out for ourselves. I can't promise you that life will be all roses and butterflies, but I can promise you that you find yourself a lot happier if, like Frank Stitt teaches us in an earlier chapter, you are able to connect with the work. This is an ever-changing process that never really goes away. That is, unless you decide to throw in the towel and decide to make the decisions for your life based on what other people might think.

Though, I can't guarantee you success, I can promise you that as long as you are trying new things, attempting to understand the way your work and the world operates, than you will constantly find yourself growing into the person that you need to become. It takes asking questions, taking chance,s and putting yourself out there in the same way that Dominique Crenn did. She was a

French woman with no restaurant experience, who would ever have considered her to be qualified? No one.

Jeremiah Tower owned and operated Stars restaurant in San Francisco after leaving Alice Waters at Chez Panisse. One day a young man came in for lunch by himself, enjoyed his meal and was gone. He did the same thing the following day, and the next and the next. Finally on the fourth day Chef Tower went up to his table and jokingly asked,

"Are you a spy for Wolfgang Puck, or what?"

"No sir, I'm not. I want to work with you. I want a job."

Tower surprised responded, "Well, can you cook?"

"No I can't, but I'll do anything I can to learn."

"Okay, you're hired," Tower smiled at him.

Jeremiah Tower liked his enthusiasm and curiosity and willingness to learn from the ground up I think, in part, because someone gave him a very similar chance two decades prior. Tower has been quite a polarizing figure in the world of American gastronomy, however, there's no arguing the magnitude of his impact across the entire industry. As a freshly graduated student from Harvard's architectural design program, Tower started making his way across the country toward the Pacific Ocean with his eyes set on a career in underwater architecture in Hawaii. He stopped in the San Francisco area en route to that beautiful volcanic cluster of islands that sit deep in the heart of the ocean and decided to stay for a bit. His grandfather, who'd been supporting him at the time, passed away and young Jeremiah (nearly thirty at this point, ha) realized he only had twenty five dollars to his name and quickly had to get a job. Staying with a friend from college who referred him to a job opening at Chez Panisse that was advertised in the paper, Tower decided to take him up on the suggestion. The "Help Wanted" ad said to stop by the restaurant at six o'clock, so Tower took the bus, a seven dollar and fifty cent round-trip ticket, into Berkeley and showed up as instructed, at six.

"What are you doing here? It's six o' clock and we're about to start service. Come back at a different time."

Tower started to walk out, feeling defeated and decided he couldn't just waste this precious, dwindling supply of pocket change on an unsuccessful trip across town, turned around, and walked right back into the kitchen.

"Your ad said to come in six. Here I am goddamnit!"

The proprietor, the now famous Alice Waters, told him to find some work to do and mentioned that there was a soup that might need fixing.

He fixed it and was hired as the executive chef of Chez Panisse. That was the first time Jeremiah Tower stepped foot into a restaurant kitchen. A year later he became equal partners with Waters and her partners and stayed there until 1978, citing irreconcilable differences as the reason for his departure. If you're a young cook you've probably never heard of Jeremiah Tower, as he's had a somewhat controversial and volatile career, but know that he's responsible for what came to be known as California Cuisine. Sure, Wolfgang Puck had a hand in it, as did Alice Waters who had opened Chez Panisse the year before Tower arrived, but Tower is really the one that put this idea of cooking on the map. It concentrated on local ingredients, focused on the bounty of fresh produce in the California area, as well as the vast array of protein from the nearby farms, as well as the neighboring Pacific Ocean. This is where we saw, for the first time, a menu that indicated what farm or geographic area a certain ingredient came from.

By having a somewhat audacious confidence, Tower got that first job. That same confidence allowed him to grow into the chef who would go on to become one of the first celebrity chefs in the world. Before garnering any real fame or attention, he brought awareness to Waters' restaurant, until differences led him to Los

Angeles where he opened Stars Restaurant. Stars was the first restaurant in the country with an open kitchen. He took the idea of fresh food and cooking, but then took it a step further and applied it to the customer experience by allowing them to truly connect with the food that was being prepared just a few feet away.

In that same kitchen, in the early years of Stars, Dominique Crenn walked in, in much the same way that Jeremiah Tower did right up the road at Chez Panisse. She had no experience working in restaurants, however, she was raised in an aristocratic family just outside of Paris by a couple of gourmands. In fact, she was eating in Michelin star restaurants as a young girl, as her father's good friend growing up was a local food critic in Paris, the culinary mecca of the world, until the last few decades. She was spoiled in the same way that Americans like to stereotype the average French family, as we assume they are raised on the finest meats, cheeses and breads in the world – she actually was. This piqued her interest in becoming a chef, but as a girl growing up in the 1970s, her parents didn't see a path for her in the culinary arts. Instead, she went to business school at Cours Charlemagne in Paris where she studied economics and international business. Once finishing and having the opportunity to create her own path, Crenn decided to move to the United States, which is when she walked into Stars Restaurant asking Chef Tower for a job. She was on the grill that night.

After working her way up, learning from the most recognized chef of his time (late 80s and 90s), Crenn decided to go out on her own and became the executive chef of a hotel in San Francisco, again, without any formal training. In 1997, the Intercontinental Hotel was opening a location in Jakarta, Indonesia and wanted to do something that was, up until then, unfathomable in a male-dominated culture like Indonesia. They wanted a female executive chef to run an entirely female kitchen. She took the job.

"It was such an amazing learning experience for me, but it was so challenging. There was so much resistance to the idea of a female chef, especially in that country, but we did it. Every single girl that worked for me that lacked confidence understood that, by the end, they could achieve great things, but it all came about because I was willing to take the chance and take the risk on this venture. Through that experience I developed so much confidence in myself, so that when I was ready to move back to the United States, I would be ready and able to do great things."

Great things she did, indeed. A few years later, she earned her first Michelin star at another Intercontinental property back in San Francisco, Luce, in 2009 and then took the chance on opening her own restaurant with no money. Atelier Crenn was bootstrapped, (something I'm all too familiar with) and opened in late 2011. It was awarded two Michelin stars the following year. The aesthetics, the menu, everything is an homage to her father and his love of art and it's beautiful. The ever-changing menu reads like a poem, because that is exactly what it is, with each line in the poem representing a different dish of their tasting menu. The beautifully crafted modernist cuisine served out of Atelier Crenn is thoughtfully comprised of California's plentiful harvest - bright colors and beautiful shapes that are created from the burgeoning use of molecular gastronomy techniques. The English translation of the word Atelier means workshop, which is exactly what she's created. The Atelier Crenn kitchen, as Dominique describes it is, "a place where people come together to share various expertise, dreams, desires, understandings and most of all, it's a place where we can all learn from each other. That's what it's all about. Everyone in the restaurant has something they can teach everyone else, and Jeremiah Tower was so instrumental in helping me to understand this. He showed me the power of giving up some control and how much it can benefit the whole restaurant. There is no screaming or yelling here. Just learning, from each other and experience."

Of all of the things I've learned from the incredibly talented and highly skilled chefs I've gushed on about over the last few pages, nothing stands out as an attribute to their successes more than their curiosities and willingness to try new things that, unfortunately, might not work.

You need to be curious, you need to create a new level of comfort that will allow you to grow – whether it's with cooking, an intimate relationship or at the gym. Sure, you can hop on the elliptical for twenty minutes a day at the same speed and resistance, I did this for years, but you're not going to really grow your muscles. If you, on the other hand, decide to go in there tomorrow and commit to exercising for thirty minutes at a slightly higher resistance, you'll tear those muscles and they will grow back stronger than they were before. Sure, you'll be sore for a few days but after a while this feeling of soreness becomes intoxicating as you realize the progress you are making in creating a healthier body for yourself. The same is true with anything we set out to do. Do we HAVE to tear those muscles? No. Do we want to? Yes, because tearing them allows us to tear them the next time and the next time and soon this idea of pushing ourselves past the limits we thought possible for ourselves becomes attractive and exhilarating and starts to feel pretty good.

I can speak from experience –every single thing that I've accomplished that has, as a result, added meaning to my life, stems from the things that I'm proud to have taken a chance on. The meaning is based on the fact that I had to put effort into achieving them. I've had to step out of my comfort zone. This process teaches us so much about ourselves that we never would have known, otherwise. Recently, I received an email from a young lady in culinary school. She's in her first year there studying, while also working part time on the line at a local restaurant. Her boss gave her the opportunity to create a special for the next weekend. With excitement, she put together a host of ingredients, followed a recipe for the most part, though veered off track from it as well, something we cooks like to do that allows us to put in our own two cents and she failed. She was heartbroken, as she realized all of her time was for naught and the ingredients were now inedible.

"Chris, have you ever screwed up so badly?"

"Of course I have, are you kidding me? I've done that probably a thousand times, that's the only way you learn. If you were only doing things you knew how to do, how would you ever get any better, right?"

I can only imagine how scary it was to move overseas as a young girl and to then walk into the hottest restaurant in town and ask the chef for a job, knowing you didn't have any cooking experience. I can only imagine how many steaks Dominique Crenn overcooked on the grill station that first night working in Jeremiah Tower's restaurant, but I know that experience helped her set the pace for incredible run in the kitchen that's been recently capped off with the honor of being awarded the "World's Best Female Chef."

When I asked Tower about that night Crenn took over the grill at Stars, back in it's prime, back when he was the culinary god of California cuisine, he said,

"She was confident and it felt right. Besides, I am a sucker for the slim chance – so far 50 percent success to 49 percent fatal tries. You live and learn, that's the industry…. That's life."

I suppose if you take enough slim chances, you are bound to create success out of one if you stick with it long enough. Either way, imagine what you might be able to learn in the process – about the work, and yes, of yourself too.

The key is wrestling with that tension of attempting something you've never done before with the fear of potentially failing in the process. Realize though, failure is part of the process. Each subsequent failure moves us closer to success. Fail enough times, feel the uncomfortableness of it, while also learning from it, and I guarantee that you'll be on to something. That's what wrestling with tension is all about – it helps develop those muscles that we need, in order to continue to grow.

"Challenges can either enrich you or poison you. You're the one who decides."
STEVE MARABOLI

THE MONKEY ON YOUR BACK

He had recently made the thousand or so mile trip down to the Jacksonville area after culinary school up in Pennsylvania. He wasn't all that familiar with what they call the "First Coast" of Florida, but his mom grew up in the area and Kenny had an uncle working close by. He earned a spot at the Ritz-Carlton of Amelia Island, where he was hired as an apprentice to work the garde manger station of the kitchen. That's where the cold items are prepared, plated and sold – salads, cold appetizers and such – the natural first rung into being graced with the opportunity to handle one's own station in a kitchen. This first rung didn't last long and by the time Kenny was 23 he had worked his way up to chef de cuisine, the person who directly reports to the chef and is essentially responsible for the maintenance of the restaurant, as their boss is typically busy frying bigger fish. During his ascension, which started as a mere apprenticeship, Kenny worked long hours – sixteen to eighteen hour days– in part because of the very seasonal and at times understaffed nature of resort work, but also because it gave him a chance to grow and learn and refine the craft. No cook goes to culinary school and gets into the business to run the garde manger station. We want to work the grill, sauté or even the more delicate craft of the saucier, but not, what many refer to as, "the cold side." Sure, there are pastry chefs and those who are destined for that type of kitchen work, but that's in their blood, and as anyone who knows the space, it's a completely different animal. So, after working the appropriate hours at his assigned station, he picked up overtime work on the butcher's block, learning more about breaking down meats that commenced as a seven year old in the suburbs of Cleveland and continued through high school with enrollment into a culinary vocational program while still going to school, which led into his years at culinary school.

In Cleveland, Kenny received a mini Weber grill as a seven year old and his parents knew something was there. He learned the basic techniques from his mother, who understood his early interest, while adopting his father's love of BBQ, smoking meats and the style with which he cooks today. In fact, we met at his restaurant, Gilbert's Underground, on the same island where he was hired as an apprentice many years before. I pulled up to the building that I knew to be a different restaurant several years prior. Inside, while waiting for Kenny who was busy pulling together a catering for the night, I learned that the young chef who was previously operating the restaurant at the same location had been lured away to a more attractive opportunity in the downtown area of Fernandina (the same island), but that fell through and left Kenny with the opportunity to open his own restaurant, something we all work toward when we decide to venture down this path of making a career out of restaurants. We met, our big rough and calloused hands shook, and he offered me some tea as we made our way to the back patio which was pleasantly shaded by the early April leaves and the shrubbery surrounding, what felt like, a back yard. This restaurant is modern and Southern, focusing on BBQ and other staples of the South, yet pulls from the various global influences that Kenny has worked with throughout his career. You can't see the smokers from the back of the building where we had begun chatting, but you can taste the smoke. He offered to show me the smokers around the side of the building lining the street, each nestled with ribs, briskets, pork butts and whole chickens that were soaking up the wonderful flavors, as well as the humidity (which keeps the meat moist during the process) that the soaked apple and hickory chips provided while slowly roasting the meat.

So, how did he get from culinary school grad and an apprentice at the Ritz, to where he is today? He's not a spring chicken, now in his mid-forties, but has created some incredible opportunities for himself. Sure, he was a competitor on Top Chef's 7th season, which has created more opportunities like the restaurant, multiple other cooking competitions including Food Network's Cutthroat Kitchen and most recently, in May of 2016, he competed and won on Beat Bobby Flay. He's cooked for Oprah several times out at her ranch in Hawaii and mingles with the best of the best along the food festival circuit throughout the country, and yes, now owns his own restaurant after a couple failed partnerships with him as chef and operating partner. I wanted to know what happened in between the years of his early twenties and where he was today. How did he get here?

When he auditioned for Top Chef, he had been working at another property owned by the Ritz-Carlton Company, but before that he had worked in Naples, Florida, for a few years and then in Sea Island, Georgia, at The Lodge overseeing the prestigious resorts' four dining concepts there and then went into consulting and catering for himself. Clearly, he had done some things right, and it wasn't just because of the fact that he could cook, that was a given. Hell, the Ritz kept calling him back. It had to be something else too, right? Our conversation that started with childhood quickly moved into the more recent, successful years, but then the conversation shifted. I asked him a question.

"So, Kenny, you've done well for yourself, but have there been any obstacles that you've had to deal with that have challenged you in a way that you weren't expecting? And, if so, what did they teach you?"

He paused, for an emotional couple of seconds.

"Sure, when I was working those early days at the Ritz, something happened that I wasn't ready for and had no idea how to handle it. I was in my early twenties, recently married and my wife and I had recently had our first child. I was young, so was she, and back then, there wasn't any of this fifteen dollar an hour minimum wage talk – if you wanted and needed to make money, you worked. So that's what I did, and that's when I started picking up extra hours at the Ritz. I had to provide for a family now. Then, one day, as the

holidays were approaching, I got a phone call. My wife was hit driving home from work. She died. She was gone.

Instantly, my world changed. I had a baby that was a few months old that I was now forced to raise by myself. I was just a kid myself. Also, the future memories of my family were occupying my mind every second of the day. That reality was shaken and taken from me in an instant, but I didn't know how to deal with it. I walked around with it for weeks and months. No one told me how to cope or manage the loss.

So then, a few months later, it was Valentine's Day. You know how Valentine's Day is in restaurants – it's balls to the walls, all hands on deck all day, running more covers than any other night the rest of the year. But, my mind wasn't right, how could it be? It was the first Valentine's Day as a widower and, emotionally, I couldn't handle it. My team needed me that night, though, and I knew it, but have you ever been in one of those funks that you can't get out of? It's all-consuming and you just can't seem to shake it? That was me. Then my boss pulled me aside, acknowledged how he thought I must be feeling, but had a conversation with me that has changed me for the better. After addressing the sensitive nature of the grief I was wrestling with, he then said 'Kenny, I need you to either pull it together or go home.'

So, I pulled it together, but only because of the way he framed it. It made so much sense to me, and it's what I preach to my staff every single day and it's what has allowed me to get to this point in my career. You see, every day you walk into work and you have challenges. We all do, that's part of life. Maybe it's bills, a fight with your spouse, your car broke down, a "friend" ripped you off. It's like a monkey that's sitting on your back weighing you down, while also playing with your head. You can bring it into work with you every day, but damn, that monkey is just baggage and keeps you from doing good work. It also keeps you from having fun while you're at work and I want you to have fun working here. Every single day for those first few months I was bringing my baggage into work with me and it was affecting everything I did, as well as the way I worked with the people around me. So he said, 'Kenny, just pretend like there's a tree right out front on your way into work. When you walk in every day, just find a limb where you can leave the monkey. Then, you can come to work and enjoy it, and leave your problems at the door, quite literally. Because, let's not forget, you'll work your shift and hopefully forget about the monkey for a while, but guess what, when you walk out that door heading home, you have to pass that tree and chances are you'll pick that monkey right back up.'

He taught me that work could be a sanctuary from the outside challenges that we all face. It could serve as a respite of sorts, and a place where I could feel safe, and I do my best to pass that lesson down to every single person that walks through these doors to work for me."

This is an earth-shattering lesson for a twenty-one or two year old to have to learn, but I have no doubt that it helped shape Kenny into the strong, kind-hearted leader and chef that he is today. What he didn't mention, though, which I think is worth noting, is that I think the analogy with this damned old monkey can be taken a step further. Sure, we all have these monkeys hanging off of our backs weighing us down, and if we can find a tree to drop them off at to play for a bit while we're inside working, great, but what I think the practice also allows us to do is to, over time, start to forget that there was a monkey even there. Slowly it allows us to adapt and realize that the monkey doesn't have to control us. Sure, it will for a while and we have to deal with whatever that monkey might be at a given point in our lives, but at the same time, as we slowly begin to let go of it, soon, we just might be able to walk out those back doors, into the parking lot and into the driver's seat, with no monkey riding shotgun. No more baggage. It allows us to let that shit go and it's liberating. Life doesn't go as planned, and we need to, after properly processing it, learn to work our ways through these challenges that we'll end up facing for the rest of our lives.

The monkey in the tree holds us back – it keeps us from doing our best work and far more impactful than that, it keeps us from being the best versions of ourselves – and I'm living proof of that. Recently, a year or so ago, I moved back to Atlanta after a six-year stint in Virginia. I moved off to chase my dreams of becoming a chef. Now, I was moving back to open up a new restaurant in the place that I'd always called home. We had a plan, a location and more importantly, investors. It was my chance to prove to everyone that I was strong, capable and a damn good chef. I could prove that, in my time away, I learned a lot and was ready to make it happen and in front of the hometown crowd.

On the day of the move, it was hot and summer's blistering heat was just around the corner. It was a nine hour trip home. With my windows down and the sunroof cracked, the GPS read just about 500 miles to Atlanta. My college CD book flapped in the breeze while riding shotgun next to me, and it was nine hours until that next chapter of my life would be underway. I could turn the pages on this challenging six years of my life. It wasn't supposed to be that way though, was it? When you start out chasing your dreams they tell you of the obstacles and hurdles that seem to show up along the way, but for me, it seemed like they popped up at every possible turn. Sure, I was starting to make a splash, whatever the hell that means, by building my personal brand, becoming a partner in a restaurant, and becoming a chef that people started to respect. I was doing TV and events and started to make a name for myself, but those are only the pieces that you see on social media or read about in a bio somewhere – you don't read about the night and day hours of putting in work when nobody is paying attention.

You don't read about the first three years of not getting paid at my restaurant, and you don't read about how I spent my life savings and the small amount of money that my mother left when she passed away, to pursue this dream and make a name for myself. You don't read about the failed relationships, the multiple times my car was towed from not being able to pay the tickets, or not being able to treat my girlfriend to a long weekend getaway somewhere, or even a nice dinner out to celebrate anniversaries and such. You don't read about that stuff, but it's there and they are the types of challenges that we all face in different forms and fashions. Finally, though, my time had come, the tides were turning and the bend in the road would open up to a straightaway and a clear shot at my dreams. So there I was, in the car heading home, for good this time, pondering my journey thus far, the choices I've made, and the ones I'd be soon making. I shuffled unlabeled mix CDs in and out of the player – the ones from college, high school and before, all taking me back to a much simpler time and place in life, but again, a sense of relief took hold of me, reminding me that there was a light at the end of the tunnel and, for the first time in my life, I could be sure that it wasn't a train coming full steam ahead. Thoughts of home and a longing for that place sent chills down my spine while cruising down those lonely southbound lanes. It would be the dead of the lonely night by the time I'd finally arrive. At least I'd be home.

I pulled into Atlanta that night and past the skyscrapers of mid-town which brightened the fog-draped sky like a row of chandeliers, glistening in the summer humidity. I decided I'd swing by the restaurant that we'd be walking through the following morning – the space we had plans of taking over, and the place where those dreams would become a reality. It had long since closed for the night, so I pulled my car right up front and into the valet circle, flipping my headlights off. I just sat in my car looking into the motionless dining room, which was just as still as the sleeping world around me. I envisioned myself with a key to the front door, a staff to manage, food to cook, and customers to make happy. In that instant, everything crystallized. I could see my future taking shape. A few short minutes turned into what felt like an hour, and I headed home a few short miles through the back roads of Buckhead.

We had the walk-through the next morning, and everything about the space felt perfect, like I'd drawn it up in my head. Our primary investor was on board, as was our real estate agent—he was thrilled for us. As excited as I was and wanted to be, I promised myself to hold it in until the deal actually went through. I wanted it in ink to avoid any disappointment like I'd experienced like a song on repeat, over and over again – it was getting old.

A week later, the day before we were planning on putting in an offer, the investor jumped ship. I understood why, and thankfully, it had nothing to do with me or us. That crystal clear picture in my mind from only a few days prior was starting to slip out of my grasp, and the picture in my head was now blurry. I'd have to figure out the next steps, but I didn't how, or what to do. Then, my business partner in the project, the day-to-day operations guy with me, he jumped ship.

I didn't even want to get out of bed, nor see anyone. Things didn't go as planned. Not in the least. They absolutely fell apart. Fuck. It stung, and it hurt. It hurt even more, because of the fact that my business partner was my brother. He had worked in various hotels throughout Atlanta running their bar programs and he was among the best in the area at doing what he did. At the same time, I knew he had that itch to give this restaurant thing a go. He had been playing it safe by taking well-paying jobs that helped pay the bills, and allowed for him to get that next job up the ladder, but perhaps, like me, he knew there was something else out there for him. The only problem is that he hadn't experienced adversity in the same way that I had. He didn't know what it was like to start and run a restaurant and how many challenges you can and will face along the way. He didn't know what it was like to work for free and grind it out in hopes of making this thing work. In fact, he and his wife at the time were trying to have a baby, a conversation he and I continually came back to – I couldn't make the decision for him, but strongly urged for him to realize the investment a restaurant takes (time, financial, emotional, etc.) and realize that maybe it's not the best time to do both. So, instead of making those sacrifices that I was hell-bent on making, in order to bring my dreams to reality, he saw the first opportunity to back out, and did so.

She ended up getting pregnant, he ended up getting a new job at another hotel and there they were picking up with their lives like nothing had ever happened. I, on the other hand, sold my share of the restaurant in Virginia (for pennies on the dollar), in order to pursue this dream in Atlanta with my brother. So, there I was

CHRIS HILL

with no restaurant plans, no income and a girlfriend who was still in Virginia, but was planning on moving down once restaurant plans were settled and finalized. I was an angry son of a bitch. It got to me big time. It affected every single part of my life. I'd lay in bed, hurt, confused and unsure of what to do next. There was a big ass monkey that slept in that bed with me every night and you could tell by the way I interacted with people. I stopped going to the gym, stopped eating healthy and couldn't seem to put any pieces together for the future.

Most of us are scared of the same thing that happened to me – it hurts. It's like a punch to the gut, when our vision and expectations don't align with what takes shape as reality. On top of that, everyone I see around town, or back in Virginia, and even on social media know why I moved back to Atlanta, so they ask about the restaurant's progress. Up until recently, I didn't know how to answer those well-intended questions – I felt ashamed, embarrassed and frankly, pissed.

It's like falling in love; you start envisioning your future with this one person, and then for whatever reason, one day your world comes crashing down – your heart is ripped out of your chest. Over time you heal, pick up the pieces, and life goes on – even if you aren't ready, and you have to explain it to the people around you, feeling like you let them down. That's where I've been, and as I put the pieces back together, I remind myself that I've been here before, and it hurts just as bad as I remember. At the same time I remind myself of the fact that anything worth having doesn't come easy, and when things don't work out, that vulnerable feeling is a primal reminder of one's aliveness and humanity. Experiencing the challenges along the way is part of what makes the story meaningful when the tides turn and the victories start rolling in, big or small.

The fear of taking a shot at anything in life lives in the fact that there are no guaranteed outcomes and this notion, sadly, paralyzes so many from ever taking a chance because they can never be certain enough. It's important to understand that the fear will always be there. That's what makes us humans, and those of us who end up leading successful and fulfilled lives have just learned to better tame and dance with that fear more than others.

If you look around, you see that we live in a world shaped, almost entirely, by people who've acted on some idea or vision for how they thought the world could be. Time and time again, we see successful people decide to show up, with a willingness to take a risk, fully aware that there's absolutely no guarantee. In fact, most of them fail more than the rest of the world even tries, which is the exact reason why they end up succeeding.

I've failed too, as much as anybody, it feels like at times, and it's been heartbreaking at times, though, this process has almost always opened the door into some of my best work. Every decision we make in life is predicated on other previous experiences that have shaped our understanding. It's the choices we make, consciously or not (and not making a choice, is itself a choice) and the potential opportunity we extract from them that ultimately write the narrative of our lives.

So it hurt. I put myself out there and fell flat on my face, but through the process I continually remind myself of how grateful I am to be alive and able to care about something so much. Most people never give themselves a chance to feel the real sting – they'd rather just sit on the sidelines.

Failure is a part of life if you hold courage as something that's important to you. You will fall down, get scraped up and your ego will bruise. It's truly opening up your heart just to see a lover walk all over it. It's hustling your face off to make the team, and getting cut in the middle of tryouts. It's starting a company, a blog, or going out for a job you really want, and experiencing firsthand how it didn't work out. It hurts, because we wanted a different outcome, but then we make it hurt even worse by creating a narrative around what has happened.

So, instead of creating that debilitating narrative, I think we're better served realizing that now we have an opportunity to pivot – to take our life in a different direction.

"Business, like life, is all about how you make people feel. It's that simple and it's that hard."

DANNY MEYER

THE ONES RIDING SHOTGUN

"Sir, let me see your license and registration please?" the cop beckoned, leaning into the brand new '77 Monte Carlo.

"Who? Officer, are you talking to me?" Duane asked, confused. "I don't think I have either of those."

"Yeah, I'm talking to you, who the hell else would I be talking to? Son, what's your name? You realize you didn't come to a proper stop at that stop sign back there?" the cop asked growing irritated.

"No sir, no I didn't. My name is Duane Keller."

"Keller, huh?" the officer smiled, "You must be the son of Ralph Keller?"

"Yessir, I am. He's out of town on a road trip and I was just heading home from hockey practice."

"Keller, follow me, we're heading to the station."

The cop wrote the thirteen year old, Duane Keller, a ticket for running a stop sign and this is how Duane made his way into the restaurant industry; he needed a job. His father, who had previously played for the New York Rangers, was currently the leading defenseman for the Hershey Bears and was away on a road trip at the time. His mother suffered from MS and was often unable to physically support the four children in the family, so Duane did what he could to get by. He learned to drive by the age of ten and was driving by himself a short time afterwards – only using the slick new ride his parents had just bought for two purposes, school and hockey practice. When his dad returned home from his road trip on the ice, Duane reluctantly informed his father of what had taken place.

"Well, son, you're going to have to get a job I suppose, you better start looking."

Duane like so many of us, myself included, stumbled into the restaurant industry by happenstance. Perhaps because of the popularity of is his last name, Keller was given a job at Alfred's Victorian, a beautiful mansion (still thriving today) in neighboring Middletown, Pennsylvania. The cuisine was inspired by the owner's northern Italian heritage. After that stint and paying off his first run-in with the law, Keller got a job at the Hotel Hershey, a huge operation with the best classically trained chefs around. Thus, Duane was exposed to the best European food and chefs in the area, all before ever graduating from high school. This propelled him in the right direction, and clearly a potential career in the kitchen was in his future, but at the same time, it's hard to overstate the impact the game of hockey has had on his life. It was in his blood. He went on to play Junior A Hockey (the minor leagues of sorts) and was drafted. However, this was still a time when hockey players, much like those of American football, weren't compensated fairly and he decided to follow his heart into cooking.

In the fall of 2015, Ralph Keller was nominated to the AHL (American Hockey League) Hall of Fame for his contribution, both on and off the ice. He was a defenseman for twenty-two years and among the leading defenders in both goals and assists, however, the true nature of a defender's mission isn't so glamorous – he or she is the last line of defense – and is also responsible for clearing the puck out of his team's half of the ice; no easy feat when the competition is also skating just as fast as they can around the rink in order to keep the puck out of your hands. As Duane and I chatted, we discussed the importance of hockey on his life.

CHRIS HILL

"Hockey and cooking are similar in so many ways, especially if you are a player-coach, the guy in charge on the ice, a role I would closely relate to that of a chef in the kitchen – they are both contact sports. You've gotta keep your head up, keep moving and communicate well. Even though you might be the leader in the kitchen or on the ice, you need to understand that you're part of a working machine and that machine stops working if one of the pieces isn't working in unison with the others. I learned from a very young age the importance of being part of this team dynamic and how hard work can take you to so many different places."

Sure, it is the team dynamic that makes things work, but how do you get there? Part of it is certainly working hard. In order to achieve what you believe to be possible for your team and for yourself, but that is also part of what earns the respect of the people around you. When they see you "digging in the corners," as Duane kept alluding to, you give them something to believe in and they see that you are out there putting yourself on the line as well. As big of a sports fanatic as I like to call myself, I can't say that I've ever been a huge hockey fan. Sure, I grew up in the South, which is undoubtedly part of it, but at the same time, I hold a slight bitterness to the NHL for when the Atlanta franchise, the Thrashers, moved back to Edmonton, where they were originally from. Let's be honest, that's where they really belong. Nevertheless, this term "digging into the corners," what the hell does that even mean? I did some research and then asked Duane and he went on to tell me how critical that player is and the amount of respect he earns amongst his teammates, based on his or her willingness to get into the thick of things. It's the guy who does the dirty work by digging into the corners to fight for the puck with the other team, and there is nothing glamorous about it, but when he's successful, he is able to wrangle the puck away from the other team, and while taking physical abuse, is able to advance the puck forward to one of the offensive stars who can then have a shot on the other team's goal. He does what his team needs him to do, in order to set them up for the best possible opportunity to be successful. It's not about credit and it's not about glory, it's about showing up every day to try to win the game. Sometimes you win and sometimes you lose, but at the end of the day, the more you put yourself in the thick of the game or the heat of battles as I'd refer to as the work in the kitchen, the better chances you have of creating success for the team as a whole.

Starting out, this is the best way to earn the respect from the people around you, and it's just by putting in the work, every single day. It's putting aside one's opportunity for personal recognition of a job well done, and doing whatever is needed for the good of the team. Restaurants, and kitchens specifically, have so many moving parts. There are so many things happening, especially as we get ready for service. Someone might be skimming the scum off the top of the veal stock that's been simmering away, but chances are, hours prior, someone else caramelized those bones and sweat down the vegetables and brought the liquid up to a simmer. Timers are always going off and if you are dicing onions, preparing your mise en place for the day and just so happen to be the closest one to the convection oven that's finishing off a crown roast of lamb, you better pay attention and you better be willing to grab a meat thermometer, check its temp, and if it's done, find the closest pair of semi-dry bar towels and take the pan out of the oven, notifying the team around you what just happened. In the middle of the rush, even if you're completely set up and ready for service when tickets start chirping through the printer, things can easily grow frantic. It's loud, the energy is high and it's hotter than hell on the line. We are stressed out and the only way to make it through is to know that the girl on your left and the guy on your right have your back. You might have to ask whoever might be least busy to make a quick run to the dry storage pantry or the walk-in, but you'll have to do the same for them later on, or perhaps tomorrow, or for your teammate on the other side. At the end of the shift, we're beat up, tired and smell like food, but the last thing on anyone's mind is actually eating any of it. It's nice, though, to be able to look around and see that things went smoothly, and that everyone pitched in where they could, not just to benefit them, or because they could, but because the entire team is de-pendent on this type of behavior from everyone. That's what it's all about, and it's how any team works – the military, on a football field, in an office environment and yes, on a hockey rink.

Since the hockey days, Duane has worked with some of the best chefs and cooked for some of the biggest names on the planet. He cooked for Julia Child's ninetieth birthday. He's cooked for presidents and diplomats and has run kitchens putting out more than ten million dollars a year in Pennsylvania, the British Columbia, Florida, and now in the D.C. area. He opened up the Gaylord National Hotel in D.C.'s Inner Harbor with 350 seats and they were doing 250K a week with an average of around a thousand covers a day.

He guided me through the preparation of a favorite appetizer off of a recent menu at his restaurant, Walker's Grille in Alexandria. It's a scallop dish that speaks right to the heart of East coast dining, while at the same time allowing for the natural flavors of the scallops to really shine. The mollusks are served in a trio, pan-seared and are served with a creamy, rich softened polenta, which is then finished off with a drizzle of lemon butter. Nothing too crazy, nothing too out of the ordinary, just good food, with integrity. Good food done right. He then rewound a recent social media conversation with a gentleman who, for lack of a better term, seemed to be barking up the wrong tree.

"Chef, what are those, scallops? How much do you charge for those anyway? Don't you know that you'll never win a Michelin star with a dish like that?"

Partly smirking internally and partly aggravated, Keller responded, before letting it go. Still audibly irritated through the phone as he told me the story, he went on to explain further.

"You think I do this to win Michelin stars? I've won plenty of awards in my day and that's the last thing I need to help me get out of bed every day. My kitchen and the work I do is grounded in the fact that our place of work is a classroom. If someone walks through the door looking for a job, has a good

attitude and is starving to learn, I'll teach them more than they'll ever learn at any of the culinary schools in the area. I always tell new hires – you get fifty screw-ups every year! You should see the relief on their face, knowing I'm not some slave-driving boss who is going to treat them like dirt like at past jobs. They get a chance to screw up, because that's how they learn, they just can't keep making the same mistake again and again."

These days, whether we work in a kitchen or in an office, we are rewired by society to chase the wrong things, the shiny objects out there in the distance, somehow thinking an award, a bigger paycheck, more restaurants or better vacations are going to make us happy and make our lives better. First of all, none of that will make your life worse, but there is nothing inherent in any sort of achievement that makes it better if it's not for the right reasons. Through all of my work personally, and by studying the greatest chefs and restaurant minds of the day, some of whom have earned those coveted Michelin stars, I've learned that the awards, the accolades, the glitz and the glamour are all very far from the point. The point is to connect to the work first and by doing that we are able to connect with the people around us, and that's where the magic happens. The magic happens when a group of guys and gals assemble in a kitchen or in an office or on the playing field, setting out on a common mission that just might be unattainable, perhaps out of reach, though, through hard work for each other and the mission just so happen to achieve their goal, or if they do fall short, they gave it one hell of a run in the process.

It's so easy to forget what's truly important, why we are here and how we are biologically wired to connect, however society seems to like to drill home the idea that we are all, in some way, in competition with each other. Social media and the pop culture world is constantly showing us the perfect lives of the people around us. Everyone offers a very stage-managed look into their lives, trying to remind everyone, in case any onlookers aren't convinced of just how great their lives actually are. This isn't what it's about, though. It's about fighting through the struggles, the adversity, and the challenges with the people around us – that's what gives us fulfillment. It's being, as my friend Adam Lamb continually preaches "in contribution." Contribution to what, though, he always asks, forcing that idea into a question we must all ask ourselves. Well, that's for you to decide, but if I know anything about the way we humans work, it's that the greatest way to feel achievement and to actually create achievement is to align ourselves with other people, to create a corner of people who have your back and you have theirs. Far greater than any Michelin stars, and I'm sure almost any chef who has owned one, are the relationships that we're able to nurture in getting there. It's about being in contribution to the work and the people around us, and it's the greatest sense of joy I've collectively gathered from all of these interviews.

It's not about you and it's not even really about the food, or the work, so much as it is about the people. Every day we have an opportunity to show up and be of service to the people around us. Wherever we find ourselves in the food chain allows us to be a mentor to somebody in some way, and then, once you've reached the top and are the one leading a team, you have an obligation to leave the people coming after you in a better situation than how you found them.

In a very long conversation with Richard Corraine, Danny Meyer's right hand man at Union Square Hospitality Group, the most coveted restaurant organization in the country, we talked about everything from Corraine's time at Cornell (the best hospitality program in the country), of his days in California working under Wolfgang Puck, and, more than anything, how much joy he's gotten out of his time with Danny and the group of restaurants they have in New York. It's no mystery to anyone remotely aware of what USHG is doing up in the Big City to understand that the driving force behind their success is their management style and strong desire to take care of their employees. As the "no tipping fad" starts to hit different pockets of the country, it's important to note that while Meyer wasn't the first to enlist this type of service, he is the one who has most certainly popularized us. As Corraine said,

∞ MAKING THE CUT ∞

"We were finding over and over again that we couldn't keep good cooks around, because they couldn't afford to stay working with us, when they could have gotten paid nearly twice as much per hour doing something else. We realized that it just wasn't fair, servers and other front-of-the-house staff was walking out every night with two, three, four hundred dollars in their pockets, while the same worker back in the kitchen works similar hours, arguably more strenuous, and walks out with a third of that. It just wasn't fair."

So, they've started implementing their no tipping system, in order to take care of their number one assets – their employees. They've found ways to minimize the impact on the employees who are in direct contact with the customers, which was a primary concern for most when the idea started to surface, but the bottom line is that there needed to be a change. Of all the companies to make a statement with this type of system that will soon be companywide, Union Square Hospitality Group seemed like the most appropriate fit. Corraine told me about the various stakeholders that contribute to their restaurants success and wasn't shy to list off their order of importance,

"First, without thinking twice about it, that's our employees, and then, in descending order it's our customers, community, suppliers and finally – investors. The whole idea that the customer comes first is BS, they can't come first. If you treat your employees with respect, integrity and empathy, then the rest kind of takes care of itself. For us, the number one skill we look for in hiring is empathy – one's ability to understand and anticipate the needs of another person, whether we're talking about a relationship with a co-worker, customer or supplier. The number one thing we, and specifically Danny, preach around here is empathy and it's at the core of our success."

If you know anything about me and my management style, you can imagine the type of connection I felt with the man on the other side of the phone. He was preaching the things I'd always appreciated and have tried putting into practice, in order to lead by example. As we chatted, I was reminded of another episode from my life – one that's both heartbreaking and hopefully encouraging at the exact same time.

I've always believed in my ability to accomplish anything I've set my mind on. If I don't know how to do something, it's time to figure it out and I've found that to never be more true than in the kitchen. Mastering a certain technique after hours of getting it wrong, or over seasoning and then under-seasoning until eventually you understand the proper amounts, and the perfect way to season a piece of meat or fish – it all comes with time and it certainly helps if you have a mentor there steering you in the right direction.

These coming of age moments in any career are hard to forget – things click into place, you finally get it and it all makes sense. It's gratifying, as you've invested time and energy into better understanding the craft. When this happens, your perspective and world view relating to your work shifts slightly. It's a fork in the road, and you're never able to see things the way you once did before. You can't.

Special moments they are indeed, but seeing and being a part of that for someone close to you? That's as good as it gets. Eric, my sous chef for two years, gave me gratification with a whole host of these moments as I saw him come into his own in the kitchen. For me, this is a perfect and continual reminder as to how much I love what I do.

The restaurant was turning the corner in its third year when Eric showed up, and quite honestly, he lacked the skills and the knowledge necessary to excel in a fast paced restaurant kitchen. I could, however, tell he wanted those things and that goes a long way in my book.

He really wanted to be good and, honestly, sometimes that's half the battle – showing up with an attitude and willingness to figure things out. I'll take that guy or girl over a technically sound, yet uninspired, cook any day of the week.

Over the first couple weeks, he began opening up about his life, which at the time wasn't a pretty picture: a recent divorce led to less visitation with his daughter, which paved the way for a weight gain of more than a hundred pounds. In those early days, pain was deep within his eyes, and understandably so, but so was a sense of fight and resolve, which are essential qualities for running the line smoothly during the rush.

Hunched over cutting boards, sweating our asses off and pumping food out as efficiently as possible is hard work and stressful, but when you look back over the course of a shift, it feels almost like things are in some sort of beautiful version of auto-pilot. You're really in the zone. You realize that nearly every movement you made was done so almost effortlessly. You've been doing the same things for so damn long, with the same people, that your body knows what to do, where it's supposed to go and how to react when necessary. Getting to this place in a restaurant kitchen, to me, is the promised land, however, if you've never experienced this, I doubt you're convinced.

The rush is exhilarating – damn, it's a lot of fun, and it is something most chefs feed off of and live for, but only if they've built a team they can trust and depend on. For us, Eric was a big part of that team and our success. Recently, we caught up and chatted about the good old days. His journey is chock full of lessons learned.

Around the end of Eric's first month working for us, we discovered a heart wrenching truth about where he was in life. He'd fallen behind on bills (I've definitely been there as well) and he was sleeping in his car. He was holding down two full time jobs – us and another restaurant. Soon after, the car was repossessed. He hit rock bottom. At this point, he had a choice to make: sleep on his buddy's couch all day feeling miserable and sorry for himself, or he could find a way to turn things around– so he did.

Success was out there for him, he just had to keep fighting. In the following months, he pulled himself out of debt, bought a vehicle, lost 80 pounds working out twice daily, and was granted more time with his daughter. He did all of this while working 70 hours a week to try to get ahead on the bills he was once behind on. His life went from night to day, and he will always be a great reminder of how hard work can, and often does, pay off. It was a joy to teach him the skills that I had to pick up on my own primarily, and through a lot of failure, he began to understand what it meant to be a professional cook, how to strategically pair flavors with one another, and what it takes to lead a team in the kitchen.

It's been fun to see Eric make his way into the mainstream core of kitchen culture – I think his military background served him well – he's used to the hard work, sacrifice and teamwork from serving two tours with the United States Army in Iraq. Of course he'd fit right in with all the ink up and down his arm. Plus, he worked in the desert, fighting a war, wearing heavy clothes and lugging a 50- pound backpack – no wonder he adapted just fine in the kitchen. Plus, as much as the typical cook talks about making sacrifices for the team, they pale in comparison to those made by the military. It's putting one's own self-interest behind fellow team members – this builds trust and a sense that they are more than just another body to fill some shoes on the line or in the field of battle. Your staff needs to know that you have their back, are invested in them, and have a sincere desire in seeing them succeed. Most managers are horribly disconnected from this idea. Most managers don't groom, nor mentor employees, they just try to keep things in order. They are just fine with the status quo, as long as it doesn't put their job in jeopardy.

A year and a half ago Eric's two year-anniversary at the restaurant came and passed as we joked about how far he had come. Probably a week later, he pulled me aside. He said we needed to talk.

Under his breath he murmured, "I have the opportunity to become the executive chef for a new restaurant in town."

"Congrats, man!" I cheered.

Sighing with relief, he went on to speak of how hard it was to build up the nerves to start that conversation. He was still petrified to break the news to my business partner and our GM – he was thinking we'd feel betrayed or mad and thought his job with us might be in jeopardy.

Like an older brother seeing a younger version of himself, I looked at Eric, started chuckling, gave him a big hug, and said,

"Dude, I couldn't be happier or more proud of you. If you need any help, venturing into these uncharted territories, I'm here to help."

It's the teaching and seeing the career and personal growth that gives me more gratification than I ever could have imagined, but, to be honest, I'd be lying if I said I hadn't learned a number of things from him as well.

Unfortunately, Eric's first stint as an executive chef didn't go as planned – I'm sure he takes some of the blame, but there were a handful of stakeholders who could probably own a stake in that as well. As things started spiraling out of control, he helplessly stepped aside and parted ways with the first kitchen he could call "his." He worked so hard to get to this point. He was bummed, and I'm sure he felt like he let me down, or if nothing else, really wanted to make me proud. To be honest, I really am. Once again, he peeled himself off the floor, swallowed his pride and found another job as the sous for a different restaurant. Having been friends and coworkers for some four years now, I'm continually inspired by the perseverance he chooses to embrace. It's hard getting knocked down and back up, over and over again. I've been there before, and there are times when I've wanted to throw in the towel and call it quits – it hurts, it's hard, and you feel like you are so backed into a corner that there is no way out. The only way out is to fight your way through, and my good buddy and sous, Eric, you are a prime example of that.

Eric and I cooked for a hundred thousand or so people together. I was able to show him the ropes, hold his hand through a very delicate chapter in his life and let him know that he didn't have to walk through it solo. It doesn't always work out so cleanly, so neat and it's not like he nor I don't have our own struggles and challenges currently – it's just a reminder that we don't have to fight those battles alone. Hell, it makes the battle something worth fighting for. We're all in it together and the second you understand this and start acting on it; your business, your relationship or wherever it is that you invest your time will start rewarding you with results

None of us are on this journey of life alone and the more we can infuse our life with the good energy of those around us, the most meaningful our own life will become. Don't forget having someone by our side, riding shotgun, makes the right a lot more enjoyable. The problem is that you need to convince them to sign up for the ride – you've got to make it worth their while, too.

"You can get everything in life you want, if you will just help enough other people get what they want."

ZIG ZIGLAR

THE SECRET NOBODY TALKS ABOUT

Leaving the gym some five years ago, almost to the day, my life changed forever. It was a beautiful day, at least in certain parts of the country. The breeze was swinging across the palm trees as the sun beamed into the oversized windows lining the front wall of the gym, and if there was a cloud in the sky, it was invisible to me. None of that mattered, though. My eyes fixated on the TV in front of me, as my phone filled with messages and phone calls. Not the phone calls you want to hear, and the types of messages you would rather just assume never existed in the first place. There, on the TV screen in front of me, were the remnants of a town I fell in love with as an 18 year old boy; an 18 year old boy who was looking for his place in the world, looking for his identity. I found a place that would sweep me off my feet and undoubtedly helped sculpt me into the man I am today. Tuscaloosa is the place that did that to me, and a piece of my heart broke the day those tornadoes killed 249 of my state mates, the ones who in some strange way were a part of my journey.

We see destruction, of all kinds every day – storms, earthquakes, disease, famines and their death tolls never really seem to go away. More often than not, though, it seems arbitrary, or if not arbitrary, distant and intangible. This could never happen to me, or the people that I love. It's intangible in the sense that, sure, it happens, but somehow we are able to distance and remove ourselves from the situation, nulling the possibility of it ever happening right before our very eyes, but then it does. Is experiencing something firsthand what makes it real to us? Is it only real and tangible if we lose our families, houses, businesses, everything we thought to have been so safe? Sure, we might not be able to fully empathize with tragedy-stricken neighbors if the tornado, hurricane or flood skips over our house and hits theirs, but isn't empathy what we more fortunate citizens are obligated to feel and, as a result, act on?

When those damned tornadoes swept through west Alabama, leveling the grounds that I studied on, the grounds where I had friends and professors and, of course, memories, it took me a few days, wrestling the idea and sadness they played over and over again on every conceivable news station in the country. The house where I lived just off of the railroad tracks off of 8th street had been wiped away and several of our would-be neighbors perished amid the howling winds. I had the opportunity to live with two of my three siblings during my year of grad school in town and some of my most precious memories took place on that rickety front porch with a bottle of wine, family and some good music playing in the background as the Alabama sun swept behind the trees to the west toward Mississippi. I spoke with several friends and my brother, Peter, who was a few years behind me at Alabama, and they were able to return to help try to make sense of the devastation that now reigned in this sleepy college town that we held so dear to our hearts. It took seeing the pictures he sent me that were of unrecognizable buildings and restaurants, all of which we frequented. It took a phone call with my good friend and professor, Buster Allaway, to check my email. There was one waiting there from him. I opened it, I sat and I cried in disbelief. Thankfully, there were no bodies, no buildings, or trees in the image he sent – it was simply a map of the area. It was two maps side by side showing Tuscaloosa pre- and post-tornado. That image will never escape my mind. In that instant, it all became too real. I knew I had to do something.

We were in the first month of the restaurant, and there was no way in hell I would be able to offer my support on the ground like so many generous people, but I knew I could do something. I could cook. So, that's what I did. I decided to throw a fundraiser in Norfolk, VA at the historic Granby Theater where I would we would sell tickets to raise money for the Red Cross of West Alabama. The event would feature my favorite DJ in town, a silent auction (which Chef Frank Stitt donated to), and my food – a southern-inspired menu of pimento cheese sliders with house-pickled okra, lima bean hummus, shrimp and grits cakes and more. In the weeks leading up to the event, I funneled whatever money I could into the event, desperately hoping for a successful night.

The evening before the event, I staked out the kitchen I'd be working out of, which was in the back of the theater and realized we had a major problem. The theater ran as a nightclub on the weekends and only offered minimal food, thus refrigeration space was limited, to say the least. Counter space was even worse, but we somehow made do. I showed up in the early afternoon hours after having to cover a no-call-no-show shift from one of our staff members at the restaurant – this put me farther behind than I ever anticipated. Even though I worked through the night at the restaurant prepping for the event, there was just too much work to do and I couldn't afford to pay my crew for the next day any more than I already was.

The rest of my crew showed up a few minutes early, just before four and I put them to work. I put Mark, my sous chef, on the grits duty, Chuck on slicing pickled okra and James, my dishwasher from the restaurant, on shrimp cleaning duty. This would keep them busy long enough to reorganize the prep list that I'd been working on continuously the last two days, but I was starting to stare right through it. I needed a break, but there was no time, we were already running behind. So, I collected my thoughts, let them finish their prep duties and pulled them all together, trying to explain how in the hell we were going to pull this off. We had insufficient burners, coolers, room for cutting boards, and no room whatsoever to plate our dishes. The marketing team that I had recently started working with on building my personal brand helped with the promotion of the event and hired a videographer as well. Throughout the course of the night, he apparently came in and out of the kitchen, but I was so head down, not even noticing him a single time. It was in the aftermath of the event that I looked at the video that was put together that I realized he was actually back there quite a bit and in every single shot you could see me dripping sweat, as if I'd just left a thirty-minute session in the sauna. It was mid-June in the American South and we were in a commercial kitchen with every possible piece of equipment cranked up to high. As I dripped sweat all over the floor, I bounced back and forth throughout the kitchen making sure all the prep was getting done. It was, and my dishwasher, James was a damn rockstar that night – that was the single proudest I've ever been seeing any of my staff working their way through a shift. He didn't know what the hell he was doing, hell, none of us did really, but he just chipped in and made magic happen wherever he could. He was brilliant.

We were expecting around a hundred people or so and the fellow hosts for the event, who were borderline worthless over the course of the night, poked their heads in to inform us that the crowd seemed bigger than expected. It was way over one hundred, seven o'clock was fast approaching and we simply couldn't get the food ready and sold? fast enough. Every time we put a new platter out, it was gone in just a few minutes. I was told that the news was outside waiting to talk to me – they were inspired by my mission to make a difference. I told them I wasn't going to be talking to anybody until everyone who paid for one of the fifty dollar tickets was happy and fed. It was the longest night of my life. If you've ever had one of those really long nights, you look back and it all just seems to be a blur, a never-ending blur. But, we made it through. I came out to say a few words, spoke with the news, and thanked all of the guests who had come out for the event. As I made my way back to the kitchen, I grabbed some beers at the bar for my crew and ached my way back into the kitchen. We did it, fellas, and though I was near the point of exhaustion and hadn't eaten all day (one of the

CHRIS HILL

great ironies of working in a kitchen), I raised my beer, clinked the mouth of mine against those of my compadres and drank the most refreshing beer of my life. Never had I felt more proud, nor more accomplished in my entire life.

We raised over ten thousand dollars for the Red Cross of West Alabama, which felt pretty good. They also named me a Hometown Hero, which was nice, as were the accolades locally, but I did it because it felt like the right thing to do. These tragedy-stricken people just wanted and needed to know that everything was going to be okay – even if it wasn't right that very second. They needed to know that their house would be rebuilt, that their businesses would somehow resurface and grow strong into the future. They needed to know that their children would have food and clothes and the basic resources we've all come to take for granted in this country. They needed to know that they would be able to provide for their families, even if they couldn't afford it. They needed to know that they could somehow return to life as normal after everything had been taken from them. Sure, some things you can't replace, but most wounds heal with time – painful, precious time. Sure enough, life does go on, and what accelerates that process is the support of those around us. It is by hope and love that we slowly rebuild these fragile lives, and these traits flow through the blood of any self-respecting chef, striving to make a difference in this world. Like most in my profession, I stumbled into chefdom, not by choice, but by an intoxicating magnetic pull that got me high off of seeing joy in people's lives. Through recipes and creating food I have the opportunity to share a sensitive and very personal side of my own life. Through this opportunity I have the opportunity every day to spark smiles, to create memories, windows of hope, and in doing so, create a world that is better for having me here. Hope and love. That is all people need in times of chaos and crisis. I have learned that I will cook with the aspiration of giving others something to hope for and cherish, and I will do so with love, for love, and to spark a smile, one meal at a time.

Through tragedy, I fell in love with cooking. I truly fell in love with it and realized the power it can have over people. Food connects people in ways I knew of, but had never experienced firsthand. The thing is, as it relates to each of the chefs I've studied over the last year, these types of fundraisers and pitching in for help whenever possible is almost understood, and I could easily write an entire book on the philanthropic nature of not just chefs, but these specific chefs. Each and every chef I connected with had their own stories to tell, their own heroic battles to fight for their community, loved ones and sometimes even for themselves. Through it all and in seeing it in my own life, it's clear that doing the *right* thing actually is the *right* thing, it also feels great to be able to contribute beyond oneself, but if that's not convincing enough, be generous with who we are is actually the right move from a business sense as well. In putting out these positive vibes, we are able to attract the type of people who believe what we believe, which is crucial in hiring, but it's also massively important in attracting the right customers for our business.

As Simon Sinek wrote in his first book – one of my favorites of all time –*Start With Why,* "people don't but what you do, they buy why you do it." Thus, people aren't buying food, or a piece of jewelry, or whatever it is we sell (well, technically they are), they are buying what our company and brands represent. I'm convinced that the entire reason I've been able to attract an audience in the restaurant world is because of the fact that I clearly articulate what it is that I do. All sorts of people cook, but very few attempt to tackle the topics in the same way that I do. It's the same reason why Duane Keller has a killer staff that would go to war for him, it's the same reason why Dominique Crenn was the first female chef in the United States to earn two Michelin stars, and it's the same reason why Gavin Kaysen was able to relocate from New York back home to Minneapolis – people knew who he was and what he represented.

There are problems with this, though. It goes back to the idea that it's a marathon, not a sprint and when business isn't great, it's easy to just cut time and corners wherever possible. The great chefs, the great ambassadors for any industry, almost always are incredibly generous every step of the way and in many cases, it's a big part of what makes them successful. You might be reading this saying to yourself, "well, I don't have any money to give, I can barely pay rent myself," and to that I would agree with you – keep your money, pay your rent first. You can, however, participate in charity events that come through your town, you can volunteer at the shelter, you can participate in citywide events that support the community. You can drive the dishwasher home on the way home from work after a long shift. It doesn't matter how you give back, but I can tell you, chipping in here and there along the way is, without a doubt, one of the prerequisites to achieving this success status we're all after – not because it will make you more money, but because of the fact that no one wants to do work with a selfish person. Additionally, the long and winding road up, that beat up gravel road to where we would all call success, well, that road is long, sometimes real long, and one of the only ways to keep fighting through the long day days is to find ways to contribute beyond yourself.

The second you make it all about you is the second you've already lost. It's about people – it always has been and it always will be.

"I used to think that your calling was about doing something good in this world. Now I understand it's about becoming someone good and letting that goodness impact the world around you."

JEFF GOINS

THE REASON YOU CAN'T SKIP TO THE END

So, what *does* separate the best from the rest? What does success mean and how do we get there? I mean, it's something we're all after, but at the end of the day, when we close our eyes for the night, it's abundantly clear that most of us don't feel successful. What a bummer. I would like to think that since this book has provided an array of examples from all walks of life, that perhaps you, too, can see that success is out there for you if you really go after it.

I get it, though. Trust me, I do. We live in a society continually reminding us that success is going to school, getting a job, settling down and buying a nice house with a white picket fence in the suburbs. We live in a society that measures success by the number of zeroes in one's bank account, how many bedrooms one might have in their house and what kind of car that person might be driving. We live in a society that measures success based on social media highlight reels; we see everyone else's picture-perfect lives, while we can't help but feel stuck, feeling like our behind-the-scenes footage isn't much. All of this leaves us feeling discontent. We somehow attach our happiness and self-worth to a host of external factors that really shouldn't have any control over either. To make matters worse, as we slip into this feeling of "not enough," we seem to trap ourselves even further into this mentality that we can't change the circumstances of our lives.

So what is success? Well, here we are at the end of the book and, unfortunately, it's really up to you to decide that for yourself.

Some would say success is having a lot of money in the bank account, others would say it's being a good parent, others would say it's working a forty hour a week job and having the weekends free to go fishing or for playing golf. I can't tell you what success means to you, but I can tell you that I firmly believe it's rooted in fulfillment.

This might disappoint some, but it's nice to know that fulfillment has very little to do with the outside world and has almost everything to do with the kind of satisfaction we have when we close our eyes at night and the excitement in our step when we hop out of bed for the day. Fulfillment is something each of us decides on our own, within the confines of our own existence. However, there are two intrinsic qualities to fulfillment that, when absent, leave us longing for more.

Growth and contribution. Each of the stories you've read in getting to this point in the book circle back around to these two ideas. It's important to be always moving towards something, to be growing into whatever it is we are hoping to become. The primary reasons why I jumped into the world of cooking was because of the fact that I wasn't growing in my work in corporate America and the actual work I was doing didn't light me up (in fact just the opposite). I was a miserable son of a bitch for that year and a half or so. As a result, I wasn't growing personally either, because I wasn't doing anything that fired me up inside. At the same time, as we grow, we realize that we are able to contribute more and more. By contributing, by seeing that the work we do and the way we spend our time, does indeed have an impact, it pushes us to want to do more of it.

Successful people, at least what most of us what deem to be successful, have a strong conviction to what they believe and see as possible, as well as their ability to execute it—to bring it into the world. They are willing to try things that might not work in order to eventually bring their vision to life, knowing that they can flesh things out along the way. To be a courageous leader takes confidence, as it's often lonely at the top. In the midst of doubt and uncertainty, however, the confident leader will almost always find a way to make it work, leaving no stone unturned. Confidence takes trusting one's gut, knowing that obstacles will arise and then being able to see the vision through. Because of this, to be the kind of leader we all admire and respect takes being mentally strong; strong enough to handle the inevitable setbacks and challenges along the way, which also breeds that certain sense of confidence within their culture as well. They are able to instill a sense of assurance and trust within their team and followers. It gives them reason enough to weather the storm, to take the risk; a risk that many might deem to be foolish. The vision allows the people enlisted in the journey to say,

"We're not sure how or why, but we trust you to get us there."

Unfortunately, failure is part of the journey toward success and throughout this book you've read numerous accounts of how various folks have been able to use to failures to move them closer to achieving what they set out to. Failure is data, and a prerequisite to achieving greatness on any level, because, by nature, trying anything new (something that's never been done before) or to step up and stand for something, requires venturing into the unknown – there is no path that leads us through the unknown. Even the most successful companies in the world have had to figure out how to get from point A to B and, along the way, face the naysayers, break through the noise, and be resilient in doing so.

Their resiliency, however, means nothing, if it's not for something greater or something bigger that these visionaries believe in, which comes down to the confidence in themselves and what their ideas represent.

I don't know your life. I don't know your struggles, nor do I know your setbacks and the walls you've had to scale along the way. I do, however, know that if you don't find something worth fighting for, something that you are confident in standing up for, you'll regret it.

The way I see it, confidence is huge, as is resiliency, and if you put those two side by side, and you'll see that they matter far more than your IQ or than the number of zeroes present in your bank account.

To believe in yourself and your ideas enough to fight through the storm, to overcome the obstacles, and to keep moving forward when anyone else would have called it quits – that's what it takes. Our most proud moments are most often born out of difficulty. Any good kitchen is going to get its ass kicked on a regular basis. In the midst of the weeds, and as the chatter of the printer seems like it will never stop, sometimes it feels overwhelming, stressful and that you are in over your head. But, like anything, the storm will pass and you will come out on the other side feeling fully alive. You can look around and say, "damn, right!" – knowing you made it, presumably together, and that you're better off for it. It's through these challenges that we grow and learn the most about ourselves. Thus, the more we submerge ourselves into situations with no guaranteed outcome, the more opportunity we have to grow through it.

So, why don't you skip to the end? Well, in the real world, you can't, and it's not even that – you wouldn't want to. The goal isn't to get to the end. The other day, I was sorting through my notes for this book as a movie played softly on the TV in front of me. I've always had a fond place in my heart for the National Lampoon's Vacation movies (every holiday season, like many across the country, we religiously pull out Christmas Vacation) and I realized that there was a modern day remake, of sorts, of the original. The only difference was that now, Rusty, the son from the rest of the movies, was the Dad and it was his turn to take the wheel, quite literally, and drive his family across the country to see Wally World. Along the way, as hilarity ensues at every possible turn (as expected), you realize that Wally World isn't the point – the point is the trip across country where the family creates these unforgettable memories that they'll laugh about ten or twenty years down the line. Finally, as the movie comes to a close and after the family has been through hell, they are able to take solace (refuge?) for the night and stay with their grandparents, the notorious Griswolds. As Rusty details the quixotic cross-country road trip, there is an exchange between Rusty and his ever-famous father, Clark Griswold. Rusty feels like a failure, like he let his family down, as he looks back on their trek across the country that couldn't have gone more wrong and is ready to just throw in the towel.

"They always say that it's not the destination, it's the journey, right?"

"The Journey sucks ... that's what makes you appreciate the destination..."

As I sat back and thought about this idea and how tweetable such a line might be, I started to think about its implications and what it really means, not just in the context of the movie, but in real life and how most of us approach our daily lives. I thought about how, when starting out and beyond, there were many times, at least for me, when things have been challenging, frustrating. There are times when I wanted to give up, fold my hands and chalk it up as a loss, but having reached a certain level of success has shown me that if you keep fighting through the challenging ride that we're all on, there is a reward. Yes, I do think that there's a reward at the end – when we're on our deathbed and our lives flash before our eyes and we look back at life in its entirety, and have something to be proud of. At the same time, I think Clark got part of this wrong. I get it, it's a cute family comedy that's not looking to have deep meaning hidden underneath each line, however, I do think that he got it wrong in saying that the journey sucks and it's all about the destination, because along the journey, however long that might be, that is where we become the people that we are today. It's important to realize that the journey is there not just to help us to get somewhere down the road, but it also molds us every step of the way – we just need to embrace it. To embrace it, I think we need to look back at the lessons these incredible chefs have taught us through their work, their lives and the lessons they've learned along the way. It's not like they got to some grandiose place and then started putting into practice these ideas of creating and implementing a vision for their lives, following their hearts, and risking their comfort level to try things they hadn't done before. They didn't start winning awards and then start appreciating the people around them, and they definitely didn't wait until then to give back through being generous with who they are. All of these pearls of wisdom have been choices that each has made along the way. These are the things that allow us to grow and contribute beyond ourselves. Embracing these ideas helps make the journey meaningful.

None of us has all of the answers, and hell, there really aren't any right answers, there's only the clues left behind from those who have come before us. At the end of the day, the clues are here to point us in the right direction, however, they don't pave the way. Each of us has to blaze our own trail and figure out the best path for our own lives. Every so often, I think it's important to stop and look around to see that we're still on the trail that we embarked upon some time ago. If somewhere along the way we look up and the trailhead is nowhere to be found and we seem to have gone painfully off track – that's okay, too. Every single day we have a choice to get back on track and when it's all said and done, it's abundantly clear that there is more than one way to get to the finish line of a life well lived. I think the most important things we need to ask ourselves out there in the forest of our lives is, am I proud of the person that I am choosing to become? Am I proud of the contribution I'm making to the world around me (whatever piece of the world we want that to be)? And finally, am I giving every single thing I have to the things that are important to me? I hope you can answer these questions without hesitation, but if not, I hope you'll have the courage to try again tomorrow and the next day and the next.

We get one shot at this thing called life.

Let's make it matter.

ACKNOWLEDGEMENTS

I've been dreaming about writing a book for years and I appreciate you spending some time with me inside these pages. If there was one word I could use to describe this experience – grateful. I'm grateful for everyone who has taken a chance on me over the years. Most importantly, Tina and my family – you all have been my rock, through the good times and bad. Dad, your support is unlike anything I knew to be possible – your belief in me is why I'm here today. My crazy siblings, Porter, Emily, Peter, Steph and Jen, as well as the in-laws – Tyler, Karina and Marko – I love all of you guys.

To everyone on social media, especially all of you guys who have been there since the early days. Back in 2011, I started my brand Bachelor Kitchen and I didn't know what the hell I was doing, but some of you guys have been around and supporting the hell out of me since those early days and have stuck with me. To all of you guys who are still around, thanks.

To Bax and Daryl, and Kat (the most wonderful GM I could have ever imagined), thanks for putting up with me through those first couple years. Ron, thanks for working your ass off every single day. Your hustle inspires me. To Vin and Josh and Stephen, y'all made living in Virginia a lot of fun.

To Jeff Goins – thanks for your guidance.

To all the podcast hosts and writers who share my work and my voice, thank you.

CHRIS HILL

A special thanks to all of the chefs and thought leaders who have contributed to the contents of this book: Gavin Kaysen, Philip Tessier, Fabio Viviani, Duane Keller, Dominique Crenn, Andrea Reusing, Jeremiah Tower, Frank Stitt, Brandon Chrostowski, Kenny Gilbert and Richard Corraine. Thank you. A special debt of gratitude to you, Adam Lamb. If I knew you could write so damn well, I'd have had you write this book for me – your foreword gives me chills every time I read it and I'm grateful to be on this mission with you, of changing people's lives for the better. It's been an absolute pleasure connecting with you these last few years. It's nice finding those people out there who just so happen to be cut from the same cloth as you.

Thank you, Mathaniel Chesson, for reaching out to me when you realized my cover art sucked. Ha. How crazy is it to think that we met on a plane a couple years ago and here we are today getting the chance to work together. I love how the world works sometimes.

To everyone who read this book and if you got this far, I assume you did – I appreciate it. More than that, though, I wish you the happiness and success in both your career and your life and hope this book might have helped you in some way in the pursuit of those things. Together, we can start changing the conversation around this industry, and a whole host of others. I can't do it alone, and neither can you, but together, I truly feel anything is possible.

Resources and Projects Referred to in the Book

Edwin's Restaurant/Institute: www.edwinsrestaurant.org
Bocuse d'Or USA/Ment'Or: www.mentorbkg.org
Southern Foodways Alliance: www.southernfoodways.org
Slow Food Movement: www.slowfoodusa.org
Chef Life Radio: www.chefliferadio.com
Restaurant Unstoppable Podcast: *www.restaurantunstoppable.com*

Also, for anyone seeking additional information regarding mental health in the hospitality industry, please check out Chefs With Issues: www.chefswithissues.com. Kat Kinsman is doing a great job to bring awareness to the restaurant and hospitality industry.

ESSAYS

The following are a series of articles and essays I've published over the last several years. People have been asking for them in some sort of printed form – this seemed like the perfect opportunity to make that happen.

These are all published personally by me and I own all rights to their redistribution.

∞ MAKING THE CUT ∞

DEAR CHEFS

They won't understand you. They won't. I know this, because I used to be on their side, stuck in a dead end office, working a shitty job, making decent pay. My family and friends were convinced I'd lost my mind when I gleefully leaped into the unknown abyss of cooking. I suppose they thought it was a phase I'd soon grow out of. Could this be you? Maybe finishing high school and are contemplating a life in the kitchen, or are already in culinary school. Maybe it's not you, but rather someone close to you. Whatever the circumstances, if you've gotten this far, I implore you to keep reading.

Chefs are a rare, often misunderstood breed and if you're amongst the naysayers, I don't blame you, I really don't, however if the smallest piece of you is debating a life in the kitchen, or have already taken that plunge finding yourself needing reassurance, you might find that here. There's also ample evidence to scare you away, there is plenty of that here. It just depends on the way your mind works.

Most will never know what it's like to make a living as a professional cook or chef, and that makes me smile. It's something of which I am arrogantly proud. No, not because I think we're better than anyone, but because of the fact that to be a really good cook or chef it takes tremendous physical, mental and emotional fortitude. Most people don't have, nor appreciate, the gifts we've been given, and this often includes our front of the house counterparts.

Seven days a week, we show up willing to get our asses kicked.
We sign up for this in exchange for an opportunity to express
ourselves through food. There's no such thing as weekends or
holidays. We might get a random Tuesday off, and if we've put in
the proper dues and happen to be in cahoots with the chef, we
just might have the good fortune of being exonerated from
working the dreaded Sunday morning brunch shift. No one wants
to work Sunday morning. We work longer days than just about
anyone. Days start early and end late, typically when the rest of
the western world is changing into their PJs, brushing their teeth
and hopping into bed. The length isn't the hard part, though, it's
the depth. Fifteen hours on your feet is grueling enough to scare
away some fence-straddlers, but on top of that, consider the
kitchen atmosphere where everything is either excruciatingly hot
or sharp as hell. Cooks scurry around cussing, the printer spewing
out tickets as fast as it can, and for hours every inch of one's
body is physically tested. Emotions are tested, and sometimes you
will fail that test. You'll break into frustration mid-shift, relying
on a teammate to help pull you through. Your mental strength
will be tested—misreading tickets, overcooking steaks,
undercooking pasta, or completely blanking the fuck out on any
number of things, once again having to rely on a teammate to
pull you through. You'll do the same for him—it's how we
survive. Close call finger-nicks and tears shed while chopping
onions don't phase us, not even secondarily. Screaming-hot 50-
pound pots of salted water simmer away, not boiling fast enough
most of the time. When the potatoes or pasta are ready to come
out, chances are a dry towel is nowhere to be found, and lacking
time to search, we somehow make do, most likely further searing
the calluses up and down our already damaged hands. Pain is an
afterthought, it doesn't faze us. It can't, or the whole ship sinks.
We owe it to the warriors next to us to keep going. There will
also be a point, mid-shift, when you'll have to make a dash to the
dry storage pantry, or the walk-in cooler. Darting across the
obstacle course of the kitchen typically includes maintaining one's
sense of balance while leaping across oil-slicked tile, dodging pans

flying in the vicinity of the dish pit, and having to weave in and out of fellow line cooks, then back into our place on the line. This is all to be done without dropping your supplies, or worse, disrupting the rhythm of the team. Disrupt the rhythm, and we all go down with you. This takes serious skills. To create the rhythm necessary for success on the kitchen line takes hours and sometimes years working together as a unit, in the trenches, slugging it out, together. Next to the military in full-fledged combat, a group of guys and gals in the kitchen know teamwork better than anyone.

Let's say you made it to the end of the service. By now, several hours have elapsed since the first tickets came chirping through the printer, and the apron draped around your neck now resembles something your dog might have chewed to hell after having splashed through the mud. You are filthy, but pots are done flying across the kitchen, flames from the burners are dulled to mere pilot lights and for the first time all night, you have a minute to breathe. A Red Bull sounds pretty good right about now, or traditionally, a cigarette in the cool fresh air outside of the kitchen hits the spot for most chefs. The burns on your hand have probably blistered already, and now that you actually have a minute, the pain hits you. The slightest of breaks and its back to business identifying prep needs for the following day. It's the easy part of the night, coasting home, after a dozen hours afoot. Now, the challenge is powering through when your mind is occupied with fantasies of beers, shots, the dive bar across the street and the pretty new waitress whose name you've already forgotten.

If there is one thing I've learned as a chef, it is that we are always learning to adapt – rolling with the punches. We put ourselves out there as artists and creators. It's a beautiful thing to have the opportunity to express ourselves through the creation of food, and the food we craft should be an expression of who we are. What we create is just as much of how the world has shaped us, as it is us shaping the way we see the world through our food. Unfortunately, most diners don't connect with our perspective. They want their food, their way, and it pisses us the hell off.

Chances are, if you aren't a chef, this has been you, and we have undoubtedly bitched about you to our fellow cooks. If you've ever put your work out into the world, you know how much it stings to have your work not appreciated as you intended. This is what keeps us up at night asking ourselves how could I do it better, and what should I have done differently? It eats at us if we let it.

Don't let it.

Chances are, your family, friends and virtually anyone close to you will be unsuccessful in understanding the life you have chosen for yourself, but maybe this letter helps just a bit. If so, they might understand why your mind is racing at 2AM after a 400 cover Friday night, and why you can't celebrate Mother's Day brunch with the fam. Perhaps now they might understand why every square inch of your body hurts most of the time, and how there really are no sick days in restaurants. They might understand why we settle for grossly underpaid wages, and hopefully they can read between the lines, and figure out why we bitch about customers upon getting off of work. They might understand how the stress from our jobs might lead us to have a few cocktails, which might be followed with a few bad decisions. Above all, if nothing else, maybe they will see that we can't imagine our lives any other way.

I'll take a handful of burn blisters, some achy knees and the hankering for a cocktail at the end of the night over ever having to sit at another desk miserably debating whether or not to shove needles through my eye balls. Living this life means we get to be creative. It means we get to showcase our skills in the heat of battle, feeling the adrenaline rush of sloshing through the trenches with guys to our left and right. These are guys we're lucky to call teammates. It means we get to be creative and stand proud for something we believe in. We get to sleep with a certain peace of mind and awaken the following morning hungry for more. Even if it means suiting up for brunch every now again, we get to make a difference in the lives of people around us in the best way we know how. We get to make them happy, and we get to do it through food.

Promise me this:

Show up every day looking to make the most of it. Learn from the best, seek to be the best, and once you are on your way, teach others to be the best. This life won't be easy. It will be damn hard, but it will be worth it, and in the end you will have lived a life of which you are proud, one that's yours, and in doing so, you get to make the world taste a bit better in the process.

COOK YOUR ASS OFF.

∞ MAKING THE CUT ∞

SO, YOU MARRIED A CHEF?

"I'm sorry. You waited up for me again last night. Work got the best of me and before I knew it, 10 o'clock was here. We got our asses kicked – we got rocked, 3 hours straight, the normal Friday night. I just saw your call, and your texts. Shit. I'm sorry. I know what you are probably thinking, with my checkered past, but believe me when I tell you, I'm sorry. I'm hustling all night, not for me, but for you, and for us—for our family. Unfortunately, at times, I know you feel like my life as a chef gets in the way of that.

I know it's hard. Maybe you knew what you were getting into, maybe you didn't. Most likely, I'd venture to say you thought you knew what you were getting into, but didn't have the slightest of clues. Right? But, if we've gotten this far together, and you haven't given up on us yet, maybe we can work through things. Keep reading and, I think, by the end you'll appreciate me, what I do, and my love for you in ways you never thought possible.

Just hear me out.

You see, I am trying to build something. Yes, I know, you are too. It's what we're all trying to do— build a life that's meaningful and that matters. Every day seems like a tug of war, though. I'm trying my best to juggle the two things that mean the most to me: our life together with that of the kitchen. They both make me feel alive. The kitchen is stressful though, god-damn it can be stressful. The hours are long and often thankless, leaving me thirsting for a few cocktails come quittin' time. Unfortunately, that can be 10 PM, or it can be 2 AM, and the crew wants me to meet them next door for a few—it's hard to say no. Regardless, though, in a way similar as to with you, I've fallen madly in love with life in the kitchen, and in some of the most unexpected of ways.

Stop, please. I know what's happening. I can see it, and I can feel it. I just don't know how to stop it. My heart breaks with yours when I see resentment lurking behind those eyes I fell in love with not too long ago, because it seems I've chosen a career you'll probably never fully understand. I get it. Your parents, they probably won't understand, and neither will your coworkers and friends. That's okay, but hopefully, by the time you finish reading this letter, you'll be proud of me, your chef. If that's the case, I hope you'll share this letter with them.

I could have gotten a high-paying job like a lot of my friends, or at least stayed with that company that provided us with a steady income. You know, as well as I, it was dead end and predictably unbearable. But you'd be right in calling it the golden ticket to a comfortable life for ourselves. Cashing in on that 401(k) sure does sound appetizing,

But, at what cost?

The weekends, the late nights, the holidays – you find yourself alone a lot. We talk about kids, but I know you tell yourself, "I don't want to raise a family alone." I get that. There is no side-stepping around those challenges and if it's not one thing, it's something else, but if you think about it, that's not just the chef life—that's life, for all of us. Life is one big storm, and we can either fight the rain, or we can learn to dance our way through it.

The obstacles, they can stand in the way, but only if we let them. The problems, some of which have been exaggerated in your head, they are real, and can bring us down, but only if we let them. The hours, the shitty pay, the potentially debilitating work environment, they can destroy us, but only if we let them. The issues surrounding a life in the kitchen have been known to wreck families and destroy fortunes, and those things, they can happen to us, but why should we let them?

You started falling in love with me—we had chemistry, and it "worked." We enjoyed spending time together, I brought you flowers, cooked you dinner, rubbed your back after a long day at the office; you noticed the small things, and I enjoyed doing them for you. You, simultaneously, could see that I was falling in love with you, and there, trust started to emerge. We respected and appreciated each other, and as things got serious, communication laid the framework, allowing trust, as well as us, to blossom into something special.

But that's not WHY you fell in love with me, that's HOW you fell in love with me, and neither my career, nor yours, should get in the way of that. You see, the reasons why you fell in love with me, and I with you—those are the same principles that have allowed me to create successful a career in the kitchen. Here are just a few of the important ones.

Communication, it's everything. It's a two way street, but it usually takes listening more, talking less, and most importantly, paying attention to the things and people around us. It's the first step toward building any relationship – intimate, working, or otherwise. In the kitchen, on a busy night, if communication breaks down, all hell breaks loose in the worst possible way. The same is true in relationships, we've all felt it, we've all been there before—it takes being vulnerable, honest and feeling terrified at times, but it's worth it every single time.

Trust is born out of honest communication. Yes, with our partners, but also with our employees and coworkers. In other words, to build anything successful in life takes authentic communication. Through that, we see that whoever it is staring back at us, working alongside us, or mentoring us – we see that they are on the same team. What a wonderful team to be on. These are the people we go to bat for, who we sacrifice for, and are the ones, to whom we, most importantly, give the benefit of the doubt to. But why? Well, it's because we trust them, and we can rely on them. Without trust, we have nothing.

Hard work, or lack thereof, I believe is why most things in this world don't work. Most failing restaurants die, not because of location or bad market conditions, but rather, because whoever's in charge, whoever that might be – they don't want it bad enough. They aren't willing work for it. The same is true in relationships – they are fun, sexy and exhilarating out of the gates, but soon passion starts to fade and most of us don't do much to keep the spark alive. Success takes fighting for something, and leaving no stone unturned when confronted with challenges along the way. It's going all-in. Hard work makes for a killer chef, businessman and entrepreneur, but makes for an even better life partner – someone who you know is at your side, always searching for ways to make things work, make things better.

Pride is showing up every single day for someone or some-thing – not because we have to, but because we want to. How good does it feel to bring your partner home to "meet the parents" or your friends for the first time? It's great, because we have the chance to brag about something we've found that makes living in this crazy world a whole hell of a lot better. Shouldn't we approach our work exactly the same way? Find work that we're head-over-heals for, and then tell the world about it? The things we've set out to accomplish, the dreams we've crafted for ourselves and the effort we put into realizing them – those things merit our pride, but just as importantly, is the pride we feel from our spouses, friends and family – the ones who support us, who walk through life with us, and see us at both our proudest and weakest moments.

Yes, it's stressful. It's hard. I bitch about customers, I complain about coworkers, at times my body hurts like hell, and after a weekend on the line, chances are I want nothing more than to sleep in for a few hours. I know it's not easy. Whether you feel like you signed up for it or not, please know that I'm doing it for us—it's what lights me up. That probably sounds selfish, and on the surface I would agree, but at the end of the day, and at the end of our lives, I'll be a much more loving husband, father and confidante if I am able to do the work I love

At the end of the day, I chose this life in the kitchen for a multitude of reasons, however, almost all of it boils down to the fact that I believed in it, found meaning through it, and most importantly I knew that it would make me happy.

Ironically, those are the same reasons why I chose and want this life with you.

∞ MAKING THE CUT ∞

IF YOU'VE EVER THOUGHT OF GIVING UP

We're all in sales.

Sure, some of us in the traditional sense, but we're also selling ourselves to future spouses, bosses and when we're trying to raise money for our startup.

If you're like me, you've heard no so many times that it's burned a hole through your ear, and fellas, you know this is true, especially in the dating world. Girls, this is why we've been terrified to talk to you since middle school. But, we've all found that guy, girl, job or project that we've set our mind on achieving, right? We've believe in it so deeply, desperately wanting it to come alive, so much so that in closing our eyes, we can see 'it' in existence? But, standing there, coming back down to reality, you open your eyes, and are reminded that it doesn't exist, and of the many hurdles standing in the way of where you are, and that thing you really, really want.

If you've seen my TEDx talk, you know I've had to deal with my own dose of adversity as an entrepreneur. I had a conversation with my Dad last night, who is incredibly supportive, and my biggest fan; probably now more than ever. We were talking about the restaurant that I'm in the process of getting off the ground, and he was asking about the various roadblocks that have shown up, the inevitable challenges that make the process so trying, and he asked,

"At what point do the obstacles and roadblocks become too much, to where it's time to put it on the back burner, and try again later?"

This is coming from a successful business man in his own right, who just hates seeing his son frustrated, and having to deal with one issue after the next. I told him,

"There is no back-burner, Dad – at least not any time soon. I'm not accepting no for an answer, I'm really not. Yeah, if I didn't believe in myself, I'd have thrown the towel in some time ago, but now? Here? No chance in hell I'm giving in..."

Maybe you've had this conversation with someone, or perhaps yourself, and it's something that I think we all have to struggle with at different points in our lives, in different capacities. We have to choose the battles worth fighting, while choosing to let go of others, but when you find that thing worth fighting for, you better give it all you've got. Going all in for a dream sounds perfect in theory, but out in the real world, it's not quite so simple. Going for something implies the risk of failure, failure leads to bruised egos, and self-consciousness, and we convince ourselves that everyone is paying attention, as we stumble and fall.

The spotlight, the place where you unequivocally stand for something can be a scary place, but it doesn't have to be. Come to terms with the fact that it's supposed to be hard. People will criticize, ridicule, and maybe even lose faith in you. I think, for me, that's an inherent part of what I've signed up for, however, in return and on the other side of adversity lies success, a feeling of accomplishment from doing something meaningful, and a sense of pride at having stuck with it, when I could have just called it quits.

But, you have to keep going.

Eventually, you'll start hearing yes, you see that the challenges and difficulties are part of what make it meaningful, and celebrate the fact that not just anyone could have done it. It takes thick skin, though, a healthy dose of grit, and some determination (all of which can be learned), because it's easy to give in and it's easy to give up...unless you've found something worth fighting for.

So, I'm convinced, the first step in the journey is finding that thing you're ready to fight for, and willing to lose sleep over – you can't get it out of your head. The fact is, any project worth its salt is going to require a fight, a loss of sleep and a developed ability to say yes when the world, the market, the girl, are all telling you no. It's easy to accept no as the answer, most of us do, unless we've committed ourselves to saying yes. We watch people join the gym every New Year, only to see them quit six weeks later (gotta love it once the gym starts clearing out again), and we watch couples commit to one another through marriage vows, only to watch it dissolve a few years later. But, it's a lot harder to skip that early January workout when you're committed to losing thirty pounds, and you're much less likely to file for divorce if you wake up every day with the commitment to making your marriage work. That's hard, though, and most of us simply don't want to put in the work. Somewhere along the way we've been conditioned to be okay with things not working out.

Convenience, in our world, almost always wins over short term sacrifice, which is almost always necessary for long term gain.

Sacrifices are necessary, in order to get what you want, and often those sacrifices show up as road blocks and hurdles that we must be willing to face, head on. Through dealing with them we get closer to where we want to be, and it's making progress even if we haven't gotten there yet. I can tell you that embracing this idea is the only way I've survived so long in the game. I've been able to use momentum as an advantage. Rejoice in small victories, and every now and then, look back and see how far you've come. I've gotten here by believing in something, and then making intentional, incremental steps toward it, knowing that each step in the right direction is moves me closer to where I want to be. As you stumble along the way, you'll see that every non-lethal failure results in another at-bat, a lesson to be learned, and another chance to get closer to what you want. So, get up there and find something to believe in, and make it happen.

Step up and swing the bat. It's going to be difficult. Difficult doesn't mean impossible, though, it just means that it's hard.

I was having a conversation with my girlfriend yesterday, who is currently living a few hundred miles away in Virginia. It's been hard on both of us, and I could hear it in her voice. She sat on the other end of the line for a minute, then said,

"Christopher, this is hard, really hard."

Pausing, I tried to find the right words to say.

"I know it's hard, it's supposed to be hard. That's how you know it's worth it."

CHRIS HILL

SCRATCH NOTES

SCRATCH NOTES

CHRIS HILL

SCRATCH NOTES

SCRATCH NOTES

CHRIS HILL

SCRATCH NOTES

SCRATCH NOTES

CHRIS HILL

SCRATCH NOTES

SCRATCH NOTES

ABOUT THE AUTHOR

Chris grew up in Atlanta, then went off to earn a Master's in Marketing that provided him with a lucrative job in consulting upon graduation that he soon learned to hate. Miserable after a year and a half, Chris made a 180° turn, followed his heart and passion into the world of cooking and opened his first restaurant at the age of 28, where he grew into the role of executive chef. Having taken his experiences in the corporate world, as well as those in the kitchen, Chris has built a large following centered around TV appearances all over the Southeast U.S., his writing, two TEDx talks and his mission of helping industry workers to lead fulfilling, successful careers. He regularly speaks and shares his work on Medium discussing topics such as restaurant leadership, overcoming failure and business/entrepreneurship.

CONTACT

For any media/speaking and any other inquiries:
Email: Chris@BachelorKitchen.com
Facebook: /ChefChrisHill
Instagram: @The_ChrisHill
Twitter: @BachKitchen and use #MakingtheCut
To Follow me on Snapchat:
1. Take a picture of the image below
2. Go into Snapchat, "Add Friends"
3. Add by Snapcode

Made in the USA
San Bernardino, CA
27 June 2017